MAKING
the MOST
of Your
COLLEGE
EDUCATION

Also by Marianne Ragins

Winning Scholarships for College:
An Insider's Guide

• MARIANNE RAGINS •

MAKING the MOST of Your COLLEGE EDUCATION

An Owl Book

HENRY HOLT AND COMPANY • NEW YORK

Henry Holt and Company, Inc.
Publishers since 1866
115 West 18th Street
New York, New York 10011

Henry Holt® is a registered
trademark of Henry Holt and Company, Inc.

Published in Canada by Fitzhenry & Whiteside Ltd.,
195 Allstate Parkway, Markham, Ontario L3R 4T8.

Library of Congress Cataloging-in-Publication Data
Ragins, Marianne.
    Making the most of your college education /
Marianne Ragins.—1st ed.
        p.   cm.
        "An Owl book."
        Includes index.
        1. College student orientation—United States.
2. Study skills—United States.   3. College students—
United States—Finance, Personal.   I. Title.
LB2343.32.R35   1996
378.1'98—dc20   96-9156
[378.1'98]   CIP

ISBN 0-8050-4404-3

Henry Holt books are available for special promotions
and premiums. For details contact: Director, Special Markets.

First Owl Book Edition—1996

Designed by Victoria Hartman

Printed in the United States of America
All first editions are printed on acid-free paper. ∞

10   9   8   7   6   5   4   3   2   1

For Gloria LaVerne Solomon
As one who truly got the most from life
and helped us to get the most from ours,
your sunny smile, loving heart and
generous ways will be remembered forever
by all of your family and friends.

Contents

Special Thanks

Patricia Cohen and the Coca-Cola Scholars Foundation; Bing Spitler, manager of college and university relations, Armstrong World Industries; Florida A & M University, and the many instructors I referenced in this book; Professor Ronald Jarrett; Dr. George Clark; Attorney William Ravanell; Dr. Ivy Mitchell; Jany Kay Allen; David Buckholtz; Angela Grant; Rondre Jackson; Otis J. Ragins, Jr.; Keasha Young; Scott Price; Cadeltra Adams; AJ Robinson; Dr. Evelyn Trujillo; Bonita Lamb, office assistant, FAMU Student Government Association; Nancy Lise, Au Pair Homestay Abroad; Dorel Drinkwine, People to People International; Gregory W. Ragins; Dr. George B. Neely; Gary P. Hritz, Association for International Practical Training; Bill Warren, The Online Career Center; Nancy R. Bailey, National Society for Experiential Education; The American Occupational Therapy Association; National Association for Equal Opportunity in Higher Education (NAFEO); National Commission for Cooperative Education; American College for Health Care Administration; Cooperative Education Association; National Education Association; Professor Tammy Hiller, Bucknell University; Professor John Miller, Bucknell University; Erin Brousseau, administrative assistant, Campus Compact, Brown University; Tracy Sherrod, my editor; and Marie Brown, my literary agent.

INTRODUCTION

Most students graduate from high school with visions of going to college but without a clear understanding of how a college education can help them. Many don't know what to expect from college, or what to expect from themselves. Some students decide to attend college at the urging of their parents; others to get away from their parents; some because of their friends; and a few for the sheer joy of higher learning. Whatever the reason, not everyone has the option of going to college. College can provide you with tremendous learning opportunities to further your personal and career development, and most other aspects of your life. However, it requires an effort and an awareness of those opportunities for you to really get the most out of it.

The total cost of a college education ranges from roughly $20,000 to $80,000 for four years. Wouldn't you consider it a waste of your money—not to mention your time—if all you did was attend classes for four or more years and then graduate, feeling no more enriched than when you arrived? Most students about to graduate and step beyond the walls of their college campus reflect on the time spent there. Some have feelings of frustration due to the realization that they have squandered four years and missed opportunities ripe with challenge and adventure. Others, who met numerous challenges and reaped the benefits of several opportunities such as an internship, study abroad, or directed individual study, feel supreme fulfillment.

Attending college can open doors into worlds otherwise unknown, as those who graduate feeling satisfied *and* enriched very well know. I have heard many college graduates exclaim, "I haven't used a thing I learned in college. The educational system is archaic. Most of my classes were boring and useless." Who wants to waste thousands of dollars and countless hours earning a degree that's useless? I'm sure *you* wouldn't want to. This book will help you get the most out of your college education, aid you in recognizing unique opportunities that you may be able to experience only as a college student or on a college campus, and urge you to take advantage of many of the resources available on your campus. When you graduate and look back on your college years, I want you to feel enriched, enhanced, and most of all that the experience was worthwhile. You will need first to understand that a college degree is not the total summation of your college experience.

Did you know that you can get college credit for volunteering in a soup kitchen or studying in London? Were you aware that you can visit a doctor, receive medical treatment, see a play, or listen to an award-winning playwright, author, or musician discuss his or her techniques in one day and in one place—your college campus? Did you know you can get investment advice or tips on starting your own business, also while on campus? For years I dreamed of learning how to play the piano, but had neither the opportunity nor the time to do it. In my last two semesters of college, I realized this dream and many more. If all you do in college is satisfy the requirements for your degree, you'll miss out on a lot of opportunities and challenges. If you don't know how you can make your college experience all you want it to be, you will after reading this book. I have written each chapter with the sole purpose of helping you get the most from your college education. I have included my experiences, those of many of my friends, and those of students at colleges and universities throughout the country to illustrate how our lives have been enriched by college. My job as author of this book is to make you aware of the many resources available at college.

Your job is to take advantage of those opportunities and use the resources available to you. You could graduate with multiple job offers in your pocket, with numerous skills and activities on your résumé, as the owner of your own business, as the possessor of an investment portfolio, as a student with many graduate or professional schools clamoring to admit you, as a world traveler, in minimal debt . . . and much more.

Without an effort on your part, college could very well be a waste of time and money. But with an effort, a world of opportunity awaits you. Explore it! Challenge it! Embrace it! But most of all, enjoy it!

Throughout your college career you will be constantly shaping your future into whatever you envision it to be. Your vision can encompass many areas. When you think of your immediate future, you may see yourself graduating, getting the job of your dreams, attending graduate school, or fulfilling your own personal fantasies. Whatever your mind conjures up for you, chances are that somewhere on your college campus or during your college career, there is an opportunity just waiting to open its doors and help you achieve your dreams. But first you must know where and how to look. You must find it, work for it, and then use it to your advantage to achieve the future you envision for yourself. If you succeed, you will have learned the true value and essence of a college education. Education has many facets and involves learning within and beyond the classroom: it encompasses the campus and its resources, your professors and their advice, your friends and their opinions, and so much more. Your overall learning experiences and your total involvement in college life differentiate the attainment of a college degree from the attainment of a complete college education.

Learning is so much more than the information in the pages of a textbook. A real college education involves tapping into every resource on campus as well as those on neighboring campuses and campuses all over the world open to you as a student. You must explore the wealth to be found in every building on your campus, in every faculty and staff member, in every contact, in every office and every club. If you do, you will be well on your way to shaping your future into the vision of your dreams and getting the most out of your college education.

If obtaining a complete college education is one of your goals, many opportunities await you. Explore many of them in this book, then explore them in reality. I promise you will be thoroughly enriched by your experiences. I know I was!

MAKING the MOST of Your COLLEGE EDUCATION

1

CAMPUS RESOURCES

On a college or university campus there are a multitude of offices and services that can assist with many of your needs and concerns. Indeed, if you know which office to consult, you may never have to go beyond your own campus. There are offices such as the career/development center to help you make career choices; launch a job search; or find a job, co-op, or internship. There are resource centers in which you can expand your leadership abilities, your writing skills, or your knowledge of mental health, for instance. If you need mental or physical treatment, you can find that too on your campus. Consult your college or university catalog for information on specific offices and the services they offer.

THE CAREER/DEVELOPMENT CENTER

The career/development center is an office or building with information and individuals dedicated to providing resources to assist you in finding both summer and postgraduate jobs, internships, cooperative education programs, study abroad courses, and much more. The career center or its equivalent should be one of the most important resources you consult when determining your career path and how you will find the job of your dreams. You should become familiar with both the reference materials in the office and the individuals who make things run smoothly. Most offices will have computers, brochures, and binders from corporate recruiters, applications, job data banks, interview sign-up sheets, lists of corporate receptions, interview dates, and a wealth of helpful information available to you as either a current student, an alumnus, or a student from a neighboring campus. At the career center you should find trained individuals skilled at helping you to determine a major, a career, and your job search criteria. They may also conduct workshops on writing résumés, successful job interviewing, taking job placement tests, completing applications, developing effective communication and networking skills, and many other topics. The career center may also offer individual counseling, career assessment tests, and videos of mock interviews. Most centers have or should have as their goals the following:

- To develop and enhance the marketability of the students who visit the office
- To provide relevant and current information to students about employment opportunities
- To expose students to corporate professionals willing and able to provide students with employment opportunities

Registering

At most career centers you will be required to register. To do so, you may need to complete a form listing your name, current address and telephone number, major, expected graduation date, times available to interview, and the types of jobs in which you are interested (internship, co-op, permanent placement). As part of the registration process you may be required to supply multiple copies of your résumé. Once you have done this, visit the office periodically for the specific purpose of updating your résumé. On the following pages you will see several variations of my résumé, including the one I created during my freshman year, primarily for internships, and the one I am currently using.

Résumé 1. Résumé used to obtain an internship and permanent job placement in the area of marketing and sales.

Résumé 2. Résumé used to apply for a job at a major public accounting firm. The recruiter was specifically interested in my coursework in accounting. By the way, this résumé attests to the advantages of hanging around the career center. I had been in the center for a while on this day after an earlier interview. The recruiter from this accounting firm saw me and started a conversation. After a couple of minutes, he asked if I would like to interview for a job in Los Angeles with his firm. I said yes. He conducted the interview and I sent him this résumé.

Résumé 3. This is my first résumé, which I used mainly for my first internship.

Although the following résumés are several pages each, your résumé should only be one page. If these were on an $8\frac{1}{2} \times 11$ sheet they would fit on one page.

Résumé 1

MARIANNE N. RAGINS

University Address	Permanent Address
FAMU Box 00000	P. O. Box 6845
Tallahassee, Florida 32307	Macon, Georgia 31208
Telephone: (904) 555-1212	Telephone: (912) 555-1212

Objective: To obtain a challenging marketing/sales position with a major corporate entity in need of an individual with extensive literary, analytical, and organizational skills.

Education: Florida Agricultural and Mechanical University—School of Business and Industry
Bachelor of Science—Business Administration
Graduation Date: April 1995
Grade Point Average: 3.8/4.0
The National Dean's List 1991–1994

Seminars/Workshops Attended: Selling Skills; Relationship Strategies; Career Workshop; Presentation Skills; Goal Setting; Writing Skills; Diversity Awareness

Honors/Achievements: Winner of over $400,000 in scholarship awards; cover story—*Parade* magazine; also featured in *Essence, Newsweek, Money, Jet, Reader's Digest, People, Black Enterprise,* and *YSB* magazines; appeared on *Good Morning America* (ABC), *The Home Show* (ABC), *Teen Summit* (BET); January 11, 1992 declared Marianne *"Angel" Ragins Day* in Wilmington, Delaware; Coca-Cola Scholar; Life-Gets-Better Scholar; Armstrong Scholar; Wendy's Scholar; Outstanding Service Award, 1991; Letter of Commendation from Clarence Thomas, Supreme Court Justice, 1991; Letter of Commendation from Thomas B. Murphy, Speaker of the House, Georgia General Assembly, 1991; Coordinator, *Benjamin D. Hendricks Undergraduate Honors Conference,* 1993 and 1994; Panel speaker, *The 21st Century—Education Beyond the Classroom,* 1993; Mock Trial Team, Florida Collegiate Honors Conference, 1992; International speaker at the Crystal Palace, Nassau, the Bahamas, 1993.

Organizations: Presidential Scholars Association; University Honors Council; Volunteer Coordinator for Special Olympics,

1991; Volunteer speaker for local schools; Red Cross Volunteer; Director of Organization and Planning, Hometown News, 1994; National Collegiate Honors Council; Southern Regional Honors Collegiate Council; Florida Collegiate Honors Council; Vice President, Junior Business Writing, Inc.; All-USA College Academic Team, 1995; Who's Who Among Students in American Colleges and Universities.

Publications: Author *and* publisher of *Winning Scholarships for College: The Inside Story*; Author of *Winning Scholarships for College: An Insider's Guide*, published by Henry Holt & Co.; Author of *Hourglass*, poetry and audio tape published by the National Library of Poetry.

Work Experience:
06/94 to 08/94
Armstrong World Industries—*Internship Assignment in Philadelphia, Pennsylvania*
Marketing Representative I
- Focused on presenting acoustical solutions to customers in the educational and health care markets of Philadelphia, Pennsylvania. Also made field sales calls for the same markets in the areas of Washington, D.C., Baltimore, northern Virginia, New York City, and northern New Jersey.
- Received the **Quality Recognition Award** for independently developing a follow-up sales call form to aid distributors and future interns with their marketing efforts.

06/93 to 08/93
EDS Belgium N.V.—*Overseas Internship Assignment in Brussels, Belgium*
Technical Assistant
- Interacted in a diverse business and personal environment composed of Belgian, Dutch, German, Irish, African, Italian, English, Spanish, and Portuguese individuals as well as many other nationalities.
- Assisted with numerous translations of Dutch, Flemish, and French into correct English grammar.
- Created financial documents and presentations for the sales, finance, and government divisions.

06/92 to 08/92
Electronic Data Systems (EDS)—*Internship Assignment in Raleigh, North Carolina*
Proposal Manager
- Entailed managing and editing material from proposal and technical writers, coordinating staff meetings and project deadlines, as well as overseeing all aspects of production concerning EDS's proposal for TIPSS.

Computer Proficiency: WordPerfect, Ventura Publisher, Lotus 1-2-3, Microsoft Word, Microsoft Excel, Microsoft Powerpoint, ABC Flowcharter, MacDraw, Photostyler, Freelance Graphics

References Available Upon Request

Résumé 2

MARIANNE N. RAGINS

University Address
FAMU Box 00000
Tallahassee, Florida 32307
Telephone: (904) 555-1212

Permanent Address
P. O. Box 6845
Macon, Georgia 31208
Telephone: (912) 555-1212

Objective: To obtain a challenging finance position with a major corporate entity in need of an individual with extensive literary, analytical, and organizational skills.

Education: Florida Agricultural and Mechanical University— School of Business and Industry
Bachelor of Science—Business Administration
Expected Graduation: April 1995
Grade Point Average: 3.8/4.0
The National Dean's List 1991–1994
G.P.A./Accounting: 3.6/4.0

Relevant Coursework: Financial Accounting, Managerial Accounting, Intermediate Accounting I, Intermediate Accounting II, Auditing I

Honors/Achievements: Winner of over $400,000 in scholarship awards; cover story—*Parade* magazine; also featured in *Essence, Newsweek, Money, Jet, Reader's Digest, People, Black Enterprise*, and *YSB* magazines; appeared on *Good Morning America* (ABC), *The Home Show* (ABC), *Teen Summit* (BET); January 11, 1992 declared *Marianne "Angel" Ragins Day* in Wilmington, Delaware; Coca-Cola Scholar; Life-Gets-Better Scholar; Armstrong Scholar; Wendy's Scholar; Outstanding Service Award, 1991; Letter of Commendation from Clarence Thomas, Supreme Court Justice, 1991; Letter of Commendation from Thomas B. Murphy, Speaker of the House, Georgia General Assembly, 1991; Coordinator, *Benjamin D. Hendricks Undergraduate Honors Conference*, 1993 and 1994; Panel speaker, *The 21st Century—Education Beyond the Classroom*, 1993; Mock Trial Team, Florida Collegiate Honors Conference, 1992; International speaker at the Crystal Palace, Nassau, the Bahamas, 1993.

Organizations: Presidential Scholars Association; University Honors Council; Volunteer Coordinator for Special Olympics, 1991; Volunteer speaker for local schools; Red Cross Volunteer; Director of Organization and Planning, Hometown News, 1994; National Collegiate Honors Council; Southern Regional Honors Collegiate Council; Florida Collegiate Honors Council; Invited to join the National Association of Educators; Vice President, Junior Business Writing, Inc.

Publications: Author *and* publisher of *Winning Scholarships for College: The Inside Story*; Author of *Winning Scholarships for College: An Insider's Guide*, published by Henry Holt & Co.; Author of *Hourglass*, poetry and audio tape published by the National Library of Poetry.

Work Experience:

06/94 to 08/94

Armstrong World Industries—*Internship Assignment in Philadelphia, Pennsylvania*

Marketing Representative I

- Focused on presenting acoustical solutions to customers in the educational and health care markets of Philadelphia, Pennsylvania. Also made field sales calls for the same markets in the areas of Washington, D.C., Baltimore, northern Virginia, New York City, and northern New Jersey.
- Received the **Quality Recognition Award** for independently developing a follow-up sales call form to aid distributors and future interns with their marketing efforts.

06/93 to 08/93

EDS Belgium, N.V.—*Overseas Internship Assignment in Brussels, Belgium*

Technical Assistant

- Interacted in a diverse business and personal environment composed of Belgian, Dutch, German, Irish, African, Italian, English, Spanish, and Portuguese individuals as well as many other nationalities.
- Assisted with numerous translations of Dutch, Flemish, and French into correct English grammar.
- Created financial documents and presentations for the sales, finance, and government divisions.

06/92 to 08/92
Electronic Data Systems (EDS)—*Internship Assignment in Raleigh, North Carolina*
Proposal Manager
- Entailed managing and editing material from proposal and technical writers, coordinating staff meetings and project deadlines, as well as overseeing all aspects of production concerning EDS's proposal for TIPSS.

Computer Proficiency: WordPerfect, Ventura Publisher, Lotus 1-2-3, Microsoft Word, Microsoft Excel, Microsoft Powerpoint, ABC Flowcharter, MacDraw, Photostyler, Freelance Graphics

References Available Upon Request

Résumé 3

MARIANNE N. RAGINS

Permanent Address	**University Address**
P. O. Box 6845	FAMU Box 00000
Macon, Georgia 31208	Tallahassee, FL 32307
Telephone: (912) 555-1212	(904) 555-1212

Professional Objective: Corporate lawyer for a major business entity that will utilize my degrees in business administration and in law

Education: Presently matriculating as a sophomore at Florida Agricultural & Mechanical University's School of Business & Industry

Relevant Coursework:
Honors English I and II
Principles of Accounting
Managerial Accounting
Introduction to Business Systems
Business Writing

Work Experience:
07/89 to 05/91
Wendy's International
Description of job duties:
- Cashier
- Elevated to gold star status in January 1991

06/92 to 08/92
Description of job duties:
- Proposal manager for the Tallahassee Integrated Public Safety System (TIPSS)
  - Desktop publishing, word processing and production for the following proposals:
    - North East Ohio Information Network (NEOMIN)
    - City of Garland (Request for Information)
    - The City of Savannah
    - The City of Broken Arrow
    - Indianapolis Sewer System

Honors/Organizations: Deans List—Fall quarter 91/Spring
quarter 92
Phi Eta Sigma National Honor Society
University Honors Council
Presidential Scholars Association
Volunteer Coordinator for Special
Olympics
Volunteer speaker for local area junior
and senior high schools
Red Cross volunteer
January 11, 1992 declared *Marianne
"Angel" Ragins Day* in Wilmington,
Delaware

References Available Upon Request

Making Your Face Known

Because the career center will be one of the most important resources on campus for finding a job you should make sure that the individuals who work there know you. Even if your campus is very large and the center sees hundreds of students a day, you would be surprised to learn how many students do not take the time to get acquainted with the center's staff. Most wait until the end of their senior year to even think about visiting the center. However, if you make it a point to stop by every week, not only to gather job information from the numerous pamphlets, magazines, and brochures in the office, but also to say hello, you will make a lasting impression, which could earn you an interview slot with a major corporation at the last minute or a personal introduction to a recruiter while you're in the office visiting. Sometimes visiting recruiters take a group of highly qualified students to dinner. One of the ways you can become one of those students is to make sure the people at the career center know who you are, since they usually recommend the students who the recruiters invite to dinner.

When to Become Acquainted with the Career Center

Although other centers may be set up differently, the career center at Florida A & M University helped students to find internships, summer programs, co-ops, and part-time employment, and assisted alumni in finding jobs. The career center on your campus may do more or less. If they do more, great! If they do less, they may be able to point you elsewhere for assistance. If they can't do that, this book is designed to help you find information on your own.

Become acquainted with the career center as early as your freshman year. Don't wait until you are about to graduate and need a job. As Whitney Young, civil rights activist, and former director of the National Urban League once said, "it is better to be prepared for an opportunity and not have one than to have an opportunity and not be prepared." Becoming acquainted with your own or another school's career center is part of your preparation for a permanent job placement opportunity or a slot in a graduate school. Not only can the career center assist you in finding a job, they can also assist you in choosing a major appropriate to your interests and goals. Many career centers do this by interviewing you or having you fill out a questionnaire. The questions asked are designed to target your primary interests and goals. Based on your answers, several majors are suggested for you to pursue. You and the career center professional then narrow it down to one.

One resource you might seek is the On-line Career Center, which can be accessed through a personal computer, a modem, and an Internet address. The On-line Career Center database has over 17,000 job listings from companies all over the country. This database can provide you with job placement information, assist you in making career choices, tell you about career fairs in your area, help launch your job search, offer résumé-writing tips, and provide other topics related your career. The database also includes company profiles. Through the On-line Career Center, you can enter your résumé into a company-sponsored database or E-mail your résumé to potential employers. For more information, contact On-line Career Center, 3125 Dandy Trail, Indianapolis, IN 46214, (317) 293-6499, or by E-mail at occ@msen.com.

Another on-line résumé database service is the Career/NET. In exchange for the required fee of $100, your résumé is sent on CD-ROM to at least 10,000 businesses, including all of the Fortune 500 corporations. Call (800) 682-8539 for more information. There are several services similar to this. However, you can probably do an adequate job of getting your résumé out without spending any money. In fact, many such services on the Internet are sponsored by employers who use the database to find potential employees and are free to the students who use them, like the On-line Career Center. Before using any database, however, be sure to thoroughly research it: If you are paying your hard-earned money, you want to know that the services can actually deliver what they promise. Ask to see an employer listing from their database. Ask your friends, relatives, and other students on campus who have used the service what they thought of it. Most important, go to your career center and ask if they have heard of the service and whether it is legitimate. For more information on the Internet, E-mail, and on-line computer databases, refer to chapter 2.

CENTER FOR SERVICE LEARNING

A center for service learning promotes volunteer service among students as a learning tool. The center may also have a learning by doing (LBD) curriculum that offers academic credit to students in exchange for community service or related activities. At some institutions, students are allowed to take advantage of an alternative semester or quarter break during which they can become immersed in a community project for one or two weeks. The time is used to confront and respond to social issues the students may have focused on only in the sterile classroom environment. Issues may include AIDS awareness, Native American culture, social justice and public policy formation, environmental issues, senior services, youth education, or homelessness.

WRITING CENTERS

Writing skills are essential in the postgraduate world. Students who have mastered the art of writing create a distinct edge for themselves over those students who have not. In virtually all careers, communication is one of the leading factors in success, and learning to write well is one of the most effective methods of communication you can acquire at college. Most universities and colleges maintain writing centers to help students improve their skills. Skilled writing consultants are on hand to help those who visit the center with revising, mastering English as a second language, identifying consistent errors, and answering general questions. Many centers conduct regular workshops on basic grammar and punctuation, preparing thesis statements, research and documentation, and critical writing techniques. Some institutions may also offer a writing center for students on-line, as does George Mason University in Fairfax, Virginia.

ACADEMIC ADVISING
OR THE ADVISEMENT CENTER

You should consult with your academic advisor about registration procedures, which courses to take, prerequisites for particular courses, your major, your career, your postgraduation plans, and any other area where you need advice and assistance. If there is one, you can also consult your school's academic advisement center. This office has professionals who aid students with issues and questions surrounding the choice of a major.

Use the following guidelines for getting the most from your advisor, the advisement center, and the advisement process.

- Be proactive. Don't wait for your advisor to contact you about registration, your major, your career, or any other decisions you must make during the course of your college career. You must make appointments with him or her.
- Use your advisor as one of your main contacts regarding such subjects as campus services, extracurricular activities, required courses, internships, and experiential learning.
- Before visiting your advisor, organize your thoughts and ideas. Write a tentative agenda for the time you plan to spend with him or her, listing all your questions. This way, you will be making the most productive use of everyone's time.
- Assess yourself and your abilities. Have at least a tentative

idea of your goals, the direction in which you want your campus life to go, your learning ability, your major interests, and your priorities.

- Become familiar with your college catalog and the schedule of classes.
- Prepare a checklist of classes that will satisfy credit requirements needed each semester or quarter. You should be able to obtain degree audits or curriculum check sheets from your advisor. Begin checking off classes that you have taken and those you still need to take and get an idea of when you would like to take the remaining courses. Your advisor will be able to help you make your selections, but remember that he or she is there to assist you—the final decisions must be yours.
- Plan—As one of my professors, George Clark, was fond of saying, "Remember the Six Ps: Prior planning prevents piss-poor performance." This is excellent advice for mastering your college experience and getting the most from it.

Before consulting the academic advisement center for help with your major, ask yourself a few questions. The major you choose could shape the rest of your life, or as many people discover, it could play a minimal role—if any. To get the most out of your college education, choose a major that in some way will positively affect your postcollegiate life. Even though learning in any form is invariably life-enhancing, it should have an impact on your eventual career. This is why you must put some serious thought into your college major. If you are already in college, you may even have to reassess the college or university you are currently attending if it does not offer a degree relevant to what you are interested in doing for the rest of your life.

In preparing for a meeting with your advisor or the advisement center, you need to consider several factors. For example: *What salary do you want to earn when you graduate from college?* Majors lead to specific occupations, and those occupations command different salaries. If salary is a primary concern to you, it should also be a primary consideration when determining your major. For example, if you major in education, your postgraduate salary might not be the same as it would if you majored in computer science. Of course personal growth, satisfaction, the thirst for knowledge, personal self-worth, challenge, fulfillment, self-respect, love, and trust can't be measured by your salary, but if you believe money and the amount of it you have are determinants of your happiness, major in an area that will command a high salary for you.

In what area will you major? Do you want a highly technical or specific major such as engineering or accounting, or a general liberal arts degree such as math or political science? General majors can be applied to many different occupations. For example, Keasha Young, a student at Florida A & M, obtained her undergraduate degree in mathematics. She is now working as a business analyst for American Management Systems (AMS). As a math major, Keasha could have pursued jobs in areas such as sales, marketing, systems management, accounting, and business management. Keasha explains: "What I do has absolutely nothing to do with math or anything I studied in my major. AMS, like many other major corporations, hires people who they think have the ability to do the job. They don't really care what your major was. They even have a guy here testing computer systems who majored in government! They'll train you in what you need to know."

I majored in business administration and I interviewed for and obtained job offers from a wide range of industries and occupations, including marketing, manufacturing, pharmaceutical sales, systems management, teaching, accounting, and consulting.

What do you enjoy doing? This may seem like a silly question, but it's one of the most important. If you don't like your major, you probably will not do well in it. Even if you do well enough to graduate with a degree in this area, you probably won't like a job in the same field. You will probably be miserable. For example, suppose you major in accounting but you hate it. You get a job with a major public accounting firm and you hate that too. You don't get promotions because your attitude stinks. You hate the fact that you haven't moved up in ten years. Because you haven't moved up in ten years, your salary reflects it. Are you getting the picture?

How much time do you want to devote to your job?　When I was in high school, my fondest dream was to become an obstetrician. I love children and I wanted to be a part of bringing them into the world. Then one of my teachers pointed out to me that babies arrive at all hours, especially odd hours like in the middle of the night, on Christmas day, at Thanksgiving dinner, or during a dinner party. She said that unless I was willing to devote a large part of my of life to my career, I probably would not enjoy my job very much. She was right. I wouldn't have—not only because of the question of time, but also because I hate the sight of blood.

If you need additional help deciding on your major, you can consult individuals at your career development center. Speak with professors and other faculty and staff to obtain additional outlooks on the subject.

THE LIBRARY

One of the most important resources that you will find on your college campus is the library. The library provides all types of information in many forms—volumes, microfilms, government documents, maps, and periodicals. They also house multimedia items such as CD-ROMs, compact discs, and interactive laser discs.

You can use the information you find for research, entertainment, classes, a business venture, or personal enhancement. For example, as a college investor you can research prospective companies in which to invest at the library. You can read daily periodicals such as the *Wall Street Journal* and *Investors Busi-*

ness Daily, or monthly publications such as *Fortune, Business Week*, and *Forbes*. You can also find *Moody's* and the *Value Line Investment Survey*. For the majority of your classes in college, you will probably have projects to complete. The library is one of the best resources for information and if you can find the perfect nook, it is also a great place for quiet study.

You may find a variety of libraries on campus tailored to certain areas of study. For example, there may be one library for business students and a separate library for law students.

Libraries on many campuses are also becoming computer friendly. Most university libraries can be accessed through your personal computer using a modem. Libraries also have computerized card catalogs, allowing easy access to information. The majority also offer computers with popular software programs such as Microsoft Word, Freelance Graphics, and Microsoft Excel in the library's media center. In most cases, the computers will also have Internet access.

If your library doesn't have information on a particular subject, it may have access to the holdings of other universities in the area. The computerized card catalog—if the library at your college has one—will also list other school's holdings. Some offer access to databases such as Lexis/Nexis and Datatimes.

THE STUDENT UNION

The student union is the most comprehensive building you will find on your university's campus. This collection of buildings, offices, services, and individuals comprises the life force of the campus. It is the community center and the focal point for virtually all student services and activities. Students can visit the student union to discuss university policies and issues with the student government president, stroll over to the cafe for a quick bite to eat, attend a meeting on women's rights, saunter into the game room for a quick bout on Streetfighter, pick up the latest brochures on dating, join the chess club, get a little money out of the bank, get a copy of John Grisham's new best-seller in the bookstore, or visit the career center and talk with a recruiter. How's that for a bastion of student activity!

Student unions usually contain the following (and frequently much more):

- Cafeteria or deli
- Lounge area
- Study area
- Game room
- Student activities office
- Student government office
- Post office
- Information desk or area
- Student organization offices
- Bank or teller machine
- Computer center
- Meeting rooms
- Ballrooms
- Career center

THE STUDENT HEALTH CENTER

The student health center offers primary health care services. University students can be examined at no additional charge for many of their health concerns. However, there is usually a fee for most tests and surgical procedures performed. Some universities also offer health and dental plans for students not covered by their parents' medical plans or by another outside plan. If needed, the health center can also prescribe medicine or provide referrals.

OTHER ON-CAMPUS RESOURCES

- Information helplines—Access to 24-hour information about the college, student resources, and events on campus
- Counseling and student development center—Offers personal and group counseling on a variety of subjects
- Drug education center—Conducts training programs and provides individual counseling; center may also have educational material such as brochures, pamphlets, and handbooks on drugs, alcohol, and substance abuse
- Health education center—May sponsor general health fairs; center may also have brochures on general health and well-being
- Campus network center—Maintains a peer educator program and offers community resource referrals; may also maintain a list of campus self-help group meetings, such as Alcoholics Anonymous
- Self-development center—Conducts workshops and provides self-instruction materials such as video and audio tapes for self-directed students. The center gives students the opportunity to develop new skills, assess themselves, or independently supplement class learning. Available programs may include stress management, anxiety control, study skills, time management, developing and handling relationships, test-taking skills, and computer skills
- Multicultural and resource center—Provides information and consultation to students and groups to promote multicultural understanding
- Child development center—Offers child care services to students, faculty, and staff; may also offer parenting workshops and learning-based programs for the children who attend
- Disability support services—Helps to integrate disabled students into campus life and academics, including assisting in the preparation of special tests, rooms, and Braille menus, or providing sign language interpreters.

- Women's studies and resource center—Holds workshops, lectures, and other events focusing on women's issues
- Center for new students—Helps freshman and transfer students make a smooth transition into the school's environment and quickly acclimates them to the campus.
- Student leadership center—Provides opportunities for students to develop and enhance their leadership skills. May offer workshops on a variety of issues and skills such as public speaking, managing others, and planning effective meetings. Excellent resource for training aids, advice, books, and media on developing leadership skills. Center may also organize conferences on topics such as women's leadership, black leadership, student leadership, and student services to honor individuals and provide a forum for discussions and insightful presentations on issues surrounding each area.

2

COMPUTERS AND
THE COLLEGE STUDENT

Ten years ago the computer was as foreign to me as a golf club. Now my computer is one of my best friends (as is the golf course). Computers are the digital present and should be familiar to every college student. On-line communication around the globe and access to enormous amounts of data can be yours at the touch of a button and the blink of a computer screen. The "information superhighway," a vast and powerful electronic network formed through the connection of telephone lines all over the world, is accessible to anyone with a computer, a modem, and a telephone line. Need a professional's opinion; want to chat with someone new; doing research? You can do it all by browsing the Internet or searching the World Wide Web.

Computers can be found in student dorms, school computer labs, co-ops, Greek houses, the library, faculty offices, and just about everywhere else on the college campus. To get the most out of your college education, learn the computer and use it. It can save time, effort, and, in most cases, frustration, and it can even be fun. The computer can be put to a limitless number of uses: for starters, you can solve complicated problems much faster than with the standard paper, pencil, and calculator; you can complete a paper and print it five minutes before class starts, if you're a procrastinator. Aspiring engineers, doctors, sociologists, mathematicians, executives, and professors all benefit from computers in their work.

For classes and majors in the disciplines of English, art, foreign languages, and psychology, computers make information easily accessible. For example, you can create databases to catalog tidbits of information. Writing papers is also easier on a word processer because it allows you to cut, paste, move, and customize your paper in any way you choose. If you need to, you can even store and retrieve papers throughout the four years and beyond.

Engineering and architectural students know the use of CAD software is essential to their studies. It's much better than relying on a drafting pencil, compass, ruler, and a straight edge to create designs and make modifications.

Some computer programs are designed to make learning a foreign language easier. If you have ever studied a foreign language, you will understand that no matter how much you practice and speak it in the classroom or even in study groups, becoming fluent will be difficult unless you actually live in a country or a region where that language is spoken. A computer armed with an immersion program guides you through real-life situations that allow you to feel like you're in the country itself, surrounded by native speakers. It may not be as effective as an actual immersion program or study abroad, but it's close. Consult your campus bookstore or software stores for more information about these language software programs.

Whether you're studying to be a scientist, mathematician, musician, journalist, computer analyst, business analyst, or a writer of cookbooks, using a computer can make your life infinitely easier. Believe me, I know. Let me profile two of my classes for you.

Class 1—In organizational behavior, I wrote at least four papers, all involving extensive research, on my computer, each approximately ten pages long. I used the computers in our campus library to search both the library's own database and the Internet for information on my topic. I printed it out, took it back to my room, and continued my literary composition without the hassle of taking copious notes, removing dozens of books from the shelves, or monopolizing a library table for six hours. I then typed the papers as they came to me, revised them at least six times, and transferred information among them in an effort to recycle some of the ideas. A bonus was that a year later, when I was asked for a business writing sample for one of my second job interviews, I easily located one of the papers on my computer and was able to submit it quickly.

Class 2—In quantitative methods II, we had to do statistical models of a problem and produce the answer using an archaic method called simplex. It involved reams of paper and hundreds of frustrating mathematical mistakes on my part, and ended up wearing down my calculator so that I couldn't see the numbers anymore. The teacher, in his infinite wisdom, wanted us to learn the process manually. Then he introduced us to a computer software program called QSB. With this program all we needed to do was map the problem, pull out key figures, input them, and presto! the problem was solved and the model was drawn, all with the touch of a button. It was great, and it saved me and my other class members at least four hours of nail-biting and headaches.

Many universities and colleges have begun to create home pages on the Internet that are accessible by students, faculty, alumni, and other users of the Internet. Depending on the institution, these electronic resources can contain information on recruiting, alumni relations, registration, class schedules and syllabi, scholarship and financial aid information, public relations, faculty and staff phone numbers, important announcements, upcoming campus and community events, and student organizations and activities. Some sororities, fraternities, student publications, societies, and other campus organizations use the Internet to generate interest in their events and communicate their purposes to students across the campus and around the world. The Internet is a great networking tool and an excellent source of information. It is an even better medium for collaborative projects that require more focused discussion than face-to-face meetings, which can often get offtrack as soon as someone mentions the last football game, wants to order pizza, or decides to watch a movie. Sitting in front of your respective computers having preliminary discussion meetings via the Internet tends to discourage goofing off.

By now I hope you understand, if you didn't already, that computers are essential to getting the most from your college studies. Not only do they save you time and thus allow you to concentrate on more exploration and research on a topic, they can also help make your classes more meaningful through real-life applications. And if you're connected to the Internet, you can find even more information about particular subjects; participate in live, on-line discussions; chat with other class members while in your pajamas; communicate via E-mail all over the world; or do extensive research without ever leaving your room. I recommend that you look into getting a computer with a modem and an Internet account. It may be one of the best decisions you ever make in college.

If you want to purchase a computer, you can find them at department stores, office stores, or computer retailers. If you know a lot about computers and feel comfortable, you can get a new or used one at a substantial discount through a mail order catalog like *The Computer Shopper*. You can purchase modems and software at any of the same places. If you need help, ask a professor who teaches computer courses to help you choose the best one for your needs (while you're at it, sign up for the professor's next course). Don't forget to ask about any student discounts on software when making your purchases. Consider software programs such as Microsoft Word, Microsoft Windows, Microsoft Excel, or Lotus 1-2-3, and Harvard Graphics or Freelance Graphics. These are the most popular software programs, and if you need to use another computer to finish a project, chances are it will have one of these programs.

A computer is a wise investment, but if you can't afford one, become familiar with those available on campus. Computers are frequently located in the campus library, media center, student union, each school or college within the university, professors' offices (if you know them well enough, they may let you use it), computer labs of particular organizations or disciplines (for example, the honors program), Kinko's or copy centers like it, and the community library.

For more information on obtaining an Internet account, consult your campus computer lab or the computer science department advisor.

If you want to go on-line and for some reason can't or don't want to do it through your campus, commercial services such as America Online and Prodigy offer consumers access to the Internet with easy-to-use graphics interfaces. America Online recently introduced College Online, an area devoted exclusively to the needs and interests of college students and professors. For example, College Online offers study tips for specific classes; tips for writing research papers; access to Compton's Encyclopedia, the Library of Congress, CNN Newsroom, and the *New York Times*; and many other features designed to make your college studies more productive and a little easier to handle.

Online Services

America Online
8619 Westwood Center Drive
Vienna, VA 22182-2285   (800) 827-6364

Prodigy
445 Hamilton Avenue
White Plains, NY 10610   (800) PRODIGY

Helpful Publications

Campus Computing
Helmut Kobler
Lyceum Publishing
2738 Parker Street
Berkeley, CA 94704

*Education on The Internet: A Hands-on Book
of Ideas, Resources, Projects, and Advice*
Jill H. Ellsworth
Sams Publishing
201 West 103rd Street
Indianapolis, IN 46290

3

NETWORKING AND
PROFESSIONAL DEVELOPMENT

NETWORKING

Networking is the process of taking advantage of all opportunities that cross your path to develop professional contacts and explore or uncover new opportunities that could result in knowledge of job leads, important business information, or trends in the market. At various points throughout your life you will have to do some networking, whether to find a job, keep a job, or further your own business. Networking can take place just about anywhere and with almost anyone. Although there are some common established places to network, such as career fairs, receptions, and so on, you can network just as easily at a friend's home, at the local gym, or in your favorite professor's office. Anytime you speak with others who have information that helps you uncover a job lead or a contact, you are networking.

Networking can help you in many ways. In addition to helping with job leads, networking can boost your confidence level and help you acquire mentors. It gives you an opportunity to exchange and receive information from individuals at many levels. As you build on your network, you can continually get advice from those you have added to the chain. You must remember, however, that networking is a two-way process, much like communication—there is a giver and a receiver, and the roles are always changing. When others assist you, they may expect something in return. If a recruiter tells you about a job opening in his company, he will expect you to be an exemplary employee for his company or certainly an interviewee who reflects well on him. If you find a mentor, she may expect you in turn to mentor someone else she recommends, or at the very least to reflect well on her by applying the knowledge or advice she has given you. If a friend gives you a job lead or contact name, some time in the future he may expect you to return the favor.

Receptions

A great way to network is by attending receptions held by corporations and organizations visiting your school. Most receptions are held the night before a day of on-campus interviewing. Getting to know your interviewer beforehand is always an advantage for you—you will be more relaxed at the interview and the atmosphere will likely have warmed from inquisitive stranger to friendly acquaintance. Also, you will be armed with more information and insight about the company and its opportunities, which can help you relate for the interviewer how your skills and experience match the company's needs.

Receptions usually last from one to three hours. They consist of a general introduction to the company by its representatives (recruiters from the company), brochures, applications, and tables of finger food. For approximately one hour, representatives will regale you with the merits of the company through a spectacular slide show, colorful transparencies, or testimonials from past interns and current employees of the company. The rest of the time is spent mingling with the representatives and with others like you, asking pertinent questions about the company, its future, and the opportunities it has to offer. If you can speak to a representative one-on-one it can be an important opening for you not only to have some of your questions answered, but to briefly describe yourself, talk a little about your background, and help him or her understand what you have to offer the company if they hire you as an intern, co-op, or permanent hire. Remember, however, that this is not an interview; give others a chance to speak, too. If you're familiar with the phrase "work the room," it definitely applies here as you repeat this question-and-answer exchange with as many of the company representatives as possible (for varied perspectives) before the night is over.

For more information on receptions, as well as a list of the receptions being held at your school or at a local hotel for students from your school, contact your career center. They'll be more than happy to help.

College Recruitment Conferences/Job Fairs

Another excellent way to develop contacts or further a job search is to attend college recruitment conferences such as those held by Careers. Each year, this Connecticut-based organization holds conferences in five major cities. They are attended by hundreds of recruiting officials from numerous companies. These conferences are almost identical to job fairs. Students are expected to dress in business attire and have copies of their résumé ready to distribute. Some companies may also interview you immediately after talking with you briefly during the conference. For more information, write to:

Careers
P. O. Box 396
North Haven, CT 06473-0395   (800) 962-3646

I first learned about this conference and other opportunities like it, including receptions, interviews, and information sessions, by reading our campus newspaper. Many companies visiting your campus will announce events they are sponsoring in your school newspaper, radio station, or TV station. Paying attention to campus media is important not only to keep abreast of campus events, but also to discover networking opportunities.

Career Fairs

Career fairs are similar to college recruitment conferences. They are generally sponsored by the individual college's career center, and are attended by recruiters from companies in various fields. Because these events are on a smaller scale (the size of your student body) there is not the clamoring for recruiters' attention that you may find at the regionwide conferences. Therefore, speaking with a representative and handing her your résumé while explaining its finer points should be much easier (unless, perhaps, you attend a huge university). Even if you are not in search of a job, career fairs are great for networking and learning more about companies in which you may later be interested. Bing Spitler, manager of college and university relations at Armstrong, says that he wishes more students would attend career fairs earlier in their undergraduate career. He feels that if they did, it would give them more time to get to know the company and for the company to get to know them and see their development over the years.

Associations

Becoming a member of or writing to associations such as the following are also ways to network, since many of the members in an association have numerous contacts in the field. They know who to call and often are in positions themselves to help you obtain a permanent job offer, get into graduate school, or win a prestigious fellowship. Contacting these organizations could result in your eventual membership if you're not a member already. Some benefits of membership you may want to consider are job leads, brochures to help you find a job or get into graduate school, information on current salaries in the field, and much more. They may also hold annual conferences which you could attend as either a member or a nonmember. If you're interested in learning which associations are related to your field of study, refer to the *Encyclopedia of Associations,* published by Gale Research. The following are a handful of the many associations that aid student job seekers.

American Institute of Certified
Public Accountants
1211 Avenue of the Americas
New York, NY 10036-8775
(212) 596-6200

American Occupational
Therapy Association
1383 Piccard Drive, Suite 300
Rockville, MD 20850
(301) 948-9626

Computer Software and
Services Industry Association
1300 N. 17th Street, Suite 300
Arlington, VA 22209
(703) 522-5055

Employment Management
Association
1100 Raleigh Building
5 W. Hargett Street
Raleigh, NC 27601
(919) 828-6614

Florida Hotel and Motel
Association
200 W. College Avenue
Tallahassee, FL 32301
(904) 224-2888

National Association of
Business Economists
1233 20th Street, NW, Suite 505
Washington, DC 20036
(202) 463-6223

National Association of Social
Workers
7981 Eastern Avenue
Silver Spring, MD 20910
(301) 565-0333

National Education
Association
1201 16th Street, NW
Washington, DC 20036
(202) 833-4000

National Paralegal
Association
10 S. Pine Street
PO Box 629
Doylestown, PA 18901-0629
(215) 348-5575

North American Telecommuni-
cations Association
2000 M Street, NW, Suite 550
Washington, DC 20036
(202) 296-9800

Public Relations Society
of America
33 Irving Place, 3rd Floor
New York, NY 10003
(212) 995-2230

Interviews

Although you may think that a job interview can have only one purpose, interviews are often an excellent source of contacts. You might interview with a company for one position but then be considered for an entirely different job within the same company or in another company or subsidiary. This has happened to me twice. I interviewed with a major banking corporation for a permanent job position. During the interview, the recruiter called in another recruiter from the company to talk to me. Months later, the second recruiter called to see if I would be interested in a position at another bank—he had left the original company but remembered our interview. Not only that, my résumé had been put in a job bank by someone else and the recruiter had recognized the distinctive border and type style I use as he was looking in the job bank for prospective candidates.

In another situation, I had a second interview, or plant visit, with a company at corporate headquarters. As is usually the case in second interviews, I met with several individuals separately. During one interview session, I was asked if I would be interested in a position in their accounting department, even though I was there as a candidate for the sales division. Although I did not choose to work for the company I had gained a unique contact during this interview. This contact would have been very helpful, had I decided to work for the company, and could still be helpful if I decided to seek a position outside my current employer.

What does this mean? It means that in every meeting you can—and should—make a lasting impression and a valuable contact. Personal contacts are invaluable when it's you and many others being considered for one position. Not only was my interview a networking situation, my résumé was also a networking tool.

Information Sessions

Information sessions are given by companies to allow students to become familiar with both the overall organization and the opportunities available. During an information session, a corporate recruiter will usually give a brief slide presentation and answer questions. Alumni from your school who are currently employed are often present to give a brief summation of their own experiences and responsibilities with the company. Past interns, co-op students, and summer employees may also be on hand to relate their experiences with the company. Such sessions are a great opportunity for you to establish a basic contact with a company or organization in which you're interested. Be sure to bring your business card (see page 36) and at least five current copies of your résumé. Hand out your business cards generously. Hoard your résumé unless you are specifically asked for a copy.

Faculty and Staff

The faculty and staff at your university are good contacts to have in your networking database. Many of them have important and sometimes powerful contacts in the world beyond your campus. They can be an excellent source for job leads, insider information, advice, referrals, or to serve as a mentor. Developing relationships with faculty and staff members is one of the first steps to creating an effective network for your on- and off-campus activities, as well as other future endeavors.

Graduate and Professional School Days

Graduate and professional school days combine the characteristics of career fairs *and* college fairs you may have attended during high school when you were deciding on which college to attend. At graduate and professional school days, as at career fairs, you are seeking information to help further your future. At graduate and professional school days, as at college fairs, you are still focusing on your future, but with a professional educational focus. More specifically, graduate and professional school days are usually sponsored by the university to provide information about specific graduate and professional programs and fellowships. Hundreds of recruiters set up booths to provide you with information about the school, the success rates of their programs, the fellowships available, and to answer your questions. Such an event allows you the perfect opportunity to develop contacts and relations with admissions officials and student representatives who could help you to gain acceptance to the program or lead to a mentoring relationship or a prestigious fellowship award.

NETWORKING TOOLS

For effective networking you need to have certain tools. Your experiences, your personality, and the impression you make are tools that will naturally follow you everywhere you go. Other tools you will need for networking include business cards, a résumé, a cover letter, an introductory letter, a follow-up letter, and computer databases. When coupled with your natural networking tools, these will make a lasting impression and can help a contact conjure up a visual picture of you.

Business Cards

You should seriously consider having business cards made. Business cards are fairly inexpensive, costing around $10 for a thousand. If you have decent computer skills and have mastered a word processing software program such as Microsoft Word or WordPerfect, you can create your own in minutes. You can then print camera-ready copy on a laser printer (if you don't have a computer or printer, use those available elsewhere on campus). After you have printed it, copy stores like Office Depot or

Kinko's will make up your cards using the camera-ready copy with which you have supplied them. The card should list your name, current address and telephone number, major, expected graduation date, and the university you attend. You may refer to my sample business card if you like. You can tailor your own business card any way you like, as long as you include the essential information.

You can buy business card forms at business supply stores like Office Depot and Staples. Using these forms, you can print your business cards yourself on your printer. Then, as changes in your address, telephone number, or graduation date occur, you can create new business cards and print them in minutes, rather than wait hours or days.

Marianne N. Ragins

Florida A & M University Undergraduate Student
Graduation: April 1995
Major: Business Administration
Degree: Bachelor of Science

Permanent Address
PO Box 6845
Macon, Georgia 31208
(912) 555-1212

University Address
FAMU Box 71470
Tallahassee, Florida 32307
(904) 555-1212

Résumé

Your résumé is the most essential networking tool you have. A résumé is a summary of your education, activities, and experiences in a concise format (most experts recommend no more than one page). Most companies considering you for a job will require one from you at some point, so keep your résumé updated. A résumé is also often required when you are applying for internships, summer jobs, co-ops, or even participating in contests. Refer to the samples of my résumés in chapter 1.

Résumés can be professionally prepared and printed by a

print shop such as Kinko's, or you can use a computer, laser printer, and heavy bonded paper to create your own. Printing your own résumé allows you the flexibility to make frequent changes. It also saves money, as having them professionally printed is very expensive, especially if you frequently make changes. Be careful to purchase envelopes in a corresponding color and weight for mailing your résumé.

Cover Letter

Prepare a cover letter summarizing key points and highlights of your résumé. You will use your cover letter when mailing your résumé to corporate recruiters and job contacts. The purpose of the cover letter is to intrigue the reader enough to look at the résumé you have enclosed and to explain the reason you are writing. In your cover letter, identify a specific position which you are interested in at the company. Tie your qualifications and background to the position. For example, if you are interested in the position of market research specialist at XYZ Company, you would highlight your position as vice president of your campus' chapter of the American Marketing Association or relevant courses you have taken, such as Principles of Marketing I and II or Marketing Management.

Introductory Letters

Introductory letters are basically "let's get acquainted" letters. They can be used in place of a cover letter to familiarize a particular contact with your name and qualifications. An introductory letter is less specific than a cover letter. In your cover letter you should be specific about the position which you are interested in and your qualifications for it. An introductory letter need only identify major areas such as marketing, finance, or sales, as shown in the introductory letter example on pages 43-44.

You may not receive a written reply right away, but if you write once a year, pretty soon they'll start to remember your name, your résumé, and your letters. If you reinforce this by introducing yourself at receptions and career fairs, you will create an even more memorable impression. Bing Spitler, manager of college and university relations at Armstrong World Industries, explains: "Not enough students come to receptions and career fairs as freshman and sophomores. They all wait until senior year or the end of their junior year to approach us and inquire about jobs. If they were to get acquainted with us earlier, it would give us time to establish a relationship and learn of each student's progress and accomplishments throughout their college career. It could give them an edge over other prospects. In my opinion, college students should focus on the job, not the degree."

Follow-up Letters

A follow-up letter such as the one shown on page 45 is another essential networking tool. Because one of the main focuses of networking is to create a favorable and lasting impression, sending a letter to thank a contact for the time she spent interviewing you, talking with you, or referring you to someone else, is just good manners. It also shows your sense of responsibility, maturity, and attention to detail. Most important, it keeps your name uppermost in the interviewer's mind and is a written reminder of your meeting.

Computer Databases

You should maintain a computer database of contact names and numbers in a spreadsheet program such as Lotus 1-2-3 or Microsoft Excel, and create mailing lists in a word processing program like Microsoft Word. As you receive business cards and correspondence from contacts or obtain names and numbers of potential contacts from friends or relatives or even a magazine article, updating your database will be easy, and all the information will be in one central location for quick and easy reference. In Microsoft Word, you can easily print your mailing list of names and addresses onto labels or envelopes.

Computer databases such as the one in the On-line Career Center (see chapter 2) can also be used to find contacts at specific companies or organizations in which you are interested. Most college campuses maintain databases such as Lexis/Nexis to aid students in their networking endeavors.

UNIVERSITY HIGHLIGHTS

The American University in Washington, D.C., is one university that delights its students with politics galore. With government internships and courses on virtually all political topics, students are immersed academically and socially in the political arena. The university maintains a network of more than 900 private, nonprofit, and government institutions. With this extensive network, the university is able to offer a wide range of subjects for its Washington Semester and co-op programs, which are open to students from other schools. All students also enjoy the benefit of having frequent speakers that most universities only dream of, such as General Colin Powell, President Bill Clinton, and Ted Koppel. Can you imagine the contacts you could make by taking advantage of the wonderful opportunities at this university? If you were in student government and in charge of arranging and organizing the booking of these speakers, for instance, or if you were involved in any of the extracurricular activities that were tied to organizing speakers, lectures, or the Washington semester and internship programs, the opportunities would be endless. Consider these: powerful contacts, in-depth knowledge of government, a network of friends who attend the Washington semester programs from universities all over the country, job opportunities, and experience and advice from the adjunct professors who work in Washington and find time to lecture on campus. The possibilities are endless.

Abbreviated Contact Listing Example

Name	Company	Department	Address 1	Address 2	City	State	Zip
	Abbot Laboratories	Manager, College Relations	Dept. 39K, AP6D	One Abbot Park Road	Abbot Park	Illinois	60064
	American Express	Human Resources	Tower World Financial Center		New York	New York	10285
Bill Cowden	American Greetings	Employment Manager	10500 American Road		Cleveland	Ohio	44144-2301
	Amoco Corporation	Human Resources Department	200 E. Randolph Drive		Chicago	Illinois	60601
	Arthur Andersen & Company, SC	Managing Director–Recruiting and University Relations	69 W. Washington Street		Chicago	Illinois	60602-3002
Brad Binder	Ashland Oil, Inc.	Professional Recruiter	PO Box 391		Ashland	Kentucky	41114

Name	Company	Department	Address 1	Address 2	City	State	Zip
Connie Rose	AT&T	College Recruiting and University Relations	100 Southgate Parkway, Room 3A02		Morristown	New Jersey	07960
Susan L. Brevoort	Banc One Cooperation			800 Brooksedge Blvd.	Columbus	Ohio	43271-0610
Gregory C. Armstrong	Bankers Trust Company			280 Park Avenue	New York	New York	10017
Doreen M. Tucker	Bellcore	Manager, Corporate Employment		6 Corporate Place	Piscataway	New Jersey	08855
Gregg A. Knowles	Chemical Banking Corporation	Vice President & Manager, University Relations	Grand Central Station	PO Box 3732	New York	New York	10163
	Chubb Group of Insurance Companies	Recruiting Coordinator			Warren	New Jersey	07059
Jim McMahon	CIGNA Corporation	University Relations	A-122, Dept. BC		Hartford	Connecticut	06152

Introductory Letter Example

PO Box 6845
Macon, Georgia 31208

December 14, 1995

Manager, College Relations
Abbot Laboratories
Dept. 39K, AP6D
One Abbot Park Road
Abbot Park, Illinois 60064

Attention: Manager, College Relations

I have read about Abbot Laboratories and its excellent opportunities in numerous career guides, magazines, and books such as *Job Choices 1995*, and *The Best Companies for Minorities*. As a result, I am very interested in working for Abbot Laboratories after graduation. My career interests lie in the areas of sales, marketing, advertising, consulting, or corporate relations.

After careful consideration, I have determined that Abbot Laboratories would offer a challenging environment for someone with my background. In addition, the business operations of Abbot Laboratories will be enhanced by the skills that I have acquired during college and summer work experience. While majoring in business administration and concentrating in the areas of finance and accounting, I have obtained a broad liberal arts background that has been supplemented by my extensive endeavors in the areas of communication primarily through writing and public speaking. As you can see by my résumé, I have authored as well as published one book and written another published by Henry Holt and Company.

I believe in stretching my capabilities to their fullest extent not only through competition, but also in service. I have participated in several competitions, spoken to numerous youth and adult groups, and served as a member of several organizations. For example, I am the winner of over $400,000 in scholarship awards. I have also been a member of the National Collegiate Honors Council, and the Southern Regional Collegiate Honors Council. Currently, I am the vice president of Junior Business Writing as well as the Chairperson for the Bernard D. Hendricks Undergraduate Honors Conference. I am also a member of the 1995 All-USA Academic Team. Furthermore, while participating in the aforementioned activities as well as many others, I have maintained a 3.8 grade point average and have been on the National Dean's List for the past 3.5 years.

Through these and many other activities I have developed extensive analytical, organizational, and communication skills. Therefore, I am certain that I would be a valuable asset to your organization.

My résumé is enclosed for your review. I would like to speak with you further about my qualifications and how they might meet your needs. If you wish to establish contact by phone, the number is (904) 555-1212.

Sincerely,

Marianne N. Ragins

Follow-up Letter

PO Box 6845
Macon, Georgia 31208

February 24, 1994

Duane H. McEwen
Group Controller
Government Contract Accounting
3M Center Building
St. Paul, MN 55144-1000

Dear Mr. McEwen:

Thank you for a pleasant and informative interview on Wednesday, February 23, 1994. During the course of our conversation I obtained considerable insight about 3M and its controller's division. I am very pleased about the interview and after reading the information you gave me upon its completion, I am even more convinced that an internship experience with your company would be an excellent opportunity. Not only could I gain significant knowledge through the experience, I have many skills which 3M could utilize as well, particularly my complementing aptitudes for using existing computer skills and swiftly acquiring new ones.

Again, thank you for the interview. I hope that you had a rewarding and enjoyable recruiting experience at Florida A & M University's School of Business and Industry. I look forward to hearing from you soon.

Sincerely,

Marianne N. Ragins

Thank-You Letter

PO Box 6845
Macon, Georgia 31208

March 4, 1994

Cheryl K. Hunt
Armstrong World Industries
Manager, College Recruiting
Organization Development
PO Box 3001
Lancaster, PA 17604

Dear Ms. Hunt:

Thank you for taking the time to speak with me on Thursday, March 3, 1994. That interview was one of the most enjoyable that I have ever had. Even though you had an extremely long day with numerous interviews, you were enthusiastic and energetic throughout the interview. Anyone who did not have an enthusiasm for sales would definitely have one after talking with you.

I am convinced that Armstrong is exactly the place for me. I am very interested in an internship position in the sales and marketing area. The extensive communication skills which I have obtained as well as my aptitudes for flexibility and creativity should definitely enhance the operations of Armstrong. I have read about the company in many magazines, and also in the book *The 100 Best Companies to Work for In America*. Armstrong is obviously an impressive company with impressive employees and products.

Once again, thank you for the interview. I hope that you had a rewarding and enjoyable recruiting experience at Florida A & M University's School of Business and Industry. Hopefully, your cold has improved by now. I look forward to hearing from you soon.

Sincerely,

Marianne N. Ragins

Networking Sources

Alumni organizations	Receptions
Civic and philanthropic organizations	Professors
Special interest groups	Classes
Sororities and fraternities	On-line databases
Churches and other religious organizations	Directories
Books and magazines	Friends
Career fairs	Career center
Graduate and professional school days	Associations

DEVELOPING INTERPERSONAL SKILLS

Developing good interpersonal skills is an important factor in successful networking and your professional development. Interpersonal skills are soft skills that most people overlook, avoid, or just don't take the time to develop. They involve the arts of writing, speaking, leadership, and related skills that can aid you tremendously in both your career and your life. They all revolve around communication and its place in your life on campus and beyond. Effective communication is one of the keys to getting what you want out of life. In most careers, it is an essential ingredient for success. If you cannot relate your ideas, stimulate understanding in others, or motivate people—including yourself—to act, you may have a difficult time realizing your visions of success.

Oratorical Skills

Learning to speak in public without twisting your tongue in knots, coming up with ways to avoid the task, or panicking is important. In today's increasingly competitive job environment, public speaking is one of the most required skills, yet it is one that people most frequently avoid developing. If you learn to do it now, you will never regret it. It will help you in day-to-day conversations, in interviews, in business, in graduate school, and in many other areas of your life, and the more you practice, the easier it will become.

To develop your oratorical or speaking skills, you should take every opportunity in college to make oral presentations, participate in oratorical contests, and engage in debates. In essence, open your mouth every chance you have (as long as it doesn't get you in trouble!) Colleges and universities are notorious for the numbers of student rallies, protests, debates, discussions, and forums they have, so your campus is one of the best places to air your ideas and thoughts.

You should have many opportunities to actually learn effective speaking skills in college. In many classes oral presentations are required. Unfortunately, many students avoid making presentations if they possibly can, just as some avoid English 101 or biology if they can. You should realize that continuous practice in classes throughout your college career may be enough to fully develop your speaking skills. Remember, practice makes almost perfect. If your regular classes do not require the oral presentation of material, you can always register for a class in public speaking or communication skills. If that still isn't enough, or you don't have the time for such a course, consider joining an organization such as the debate team, literary guild, a performing arts group, or a mock trial team. All of these organizations involve activities that require you to stand in front of an audience and speak. To help you even more, attend workshops and seminars on public speaking.

The first rule of effective communication in the art of public speaking is to be comfortable in front of an audience, however large or small—after that the rest is easy. If you practice continuously in classes or organizations, you will eventually become comfortable enough to treat your audience as a collective mass of friends instead of having to resort to the sometimes unpleasant old trick of picturing them naked. The more comfortable you are, the more relaxed you will be, which in turn will allow your thoughts to flow from your mind in an interesting and convincing stream. It makes you a very effective and often entertaining speaker.

Writing Skills

In many of your classes, particularly those in literature or with a research focus, you will be able to find a plethora of opportunities to develop your writing skills. Term papers, essays, critical reviews, and analyses will be plentiful opportunities for you to practice writing. Not only that, many of your professors may also take the time to note major errors in your writing when reviewing your completed assignments.

Another way to improve your writing ability is to visit the writing center if your school maintains one. Many colleges and universities also offer classes on technical, business, and creative writing as well as seminars and workshops to help students develop and perfect their writing skills.

Interviewing Skills

Your campus is a great place to hone your interviewing skills. For almost every activity, contest, award, position, or job you will probably have an interview, whether formal or informal. As always, the more you do it, the easier it gets and the more relaxed you will be. Relaxation and practice are great cures for stuttering, forgetfulness, and roving eyes. If this isn't enough, visit your career center and sign up for an informational interview. In an informational interview you will meet with a recruiter and talk with her just as you would in a regular interview. The only difference is that both you and the interviewer understand that the session is not intended to lead to a job. Informational interviews are another form of networking. The career center will also arrange mock interviews with professionals in the office. Or you can attend workshops, seminars, and mini-classes given by the center to aid students in the development of their interviewing skills. You could ask a professor or other faculty member—particularly one who has worked in the industry or field for which you will be interviewing—to practice interview you. Many of them will be more than happy to help you, and this will help you become more familiar with typical questions relative to that particular field or industry.

Leadership Skills

Most graduate and professional schools and employers are interested in your ability to lead, motivate, and function within a team or cooperative environment. Joining organizations and obtaining a position of leadership is one of the best ways to develop such skills. As shown on pages 96–105, there are dozens of organizations to join both on and off campus; each, in turn, offers numerous leadership opportunities. Some universities (see University Highlights, page 51) create structured student-run organizations and teach classes designed to increase students' natural leadership abilities and enhance their professional development. In many classes, teamwork is very important. As a member or a leader of a team formed in class, your leadership skills and ability to motivate others into wanting an A or some other goal are very important. Many career centers sponsor leadership workshops, seminars, and classes to help you develop leadership skills.

UNIVERSITY HIGHLIGHTS

Florida A & M University offers its students a wealth of opportunities in the area of professional development and enhancement. Many students can attest to the numerous internship opportunities all over the country, the various professional and interpersonal development programs, and other programs, such as summer research, sprinkled liberally all over the campus. Students at the School of Business and Industry are immersed from the first day in a professional development program that encompasses speed reading, technical review and analysis of business periodicals, development of oratorical skills, business writing, and, most important, leadership skills. The leadership skills are developed and honed through active participation in student-run companies, many of which have ties to the "real" world, such as Surety, Inc., where students can become certified as actual insurance agents, and the SBI Investment Fund, where, together with two financial advisers, students manage over $1 million dollars in investment capital.

4

IN THE CLASSROOM

It is easy for students to forget that time spent in class not only brings you closer to completing your major and ultimately earning a degree, it can also help you gain more knowledge than that found in the pages of a textbook. For example, as a business administration major, I took several courses that I found absolutely boring. However, since they were required courses for my major, I suffered through them. Or I suffered until I realized how much valuable information I was picking up along the way. Unfortunately, this realization didn't occur until the end of my sophomore year, but when it did, I began to make an effort to soak up information like a sponge.

You may be wondering where I am heading with this, especially since many of you probably believe a large part of the college curriculum for the first two years is core courses that can be an advanced repeat of high school. That's true. First year college courses like principles of accounting and physics, similar to those I took in high school, didn't interest me in the least until I realized that they were actually helping me. When I completed my first internship and tax time came around, I knew how to prepare my own taxes without the aid of either my parents or a tax professional. This may not sound like a big deal, but by this time I had already self-published my first book, so not only did I have income from my last internship to account for, I also had income from book sales to record. It became more than a little complicated. But with the aid of my accounting teachers, some of whom had once been practicing accountants, I sailed through them easily. Uncle Sam got his and I got back a little chunk of my own.

A college accounting course can be useful in preparing your first tax return, creating a balance sheet or income statement for a new business venture, or in calculating your net worth. If you ever need a loan for a business or other financial information, these skills are important, particularly if you can't afford a professional.

Attentive listening in an investments class could lead you to the road of sound financial management, helping you to amass a small nest egg by the time you graduate and a fortune by the time you retire. Managing your finances and investing your income are two keys to financial success. Why not take advantage of a course dedicated to it and a professor skilled in it to plan your financial future?

If you're interested, legal environment of business and commercial law are two classes that could help you with legal matters. In both classes, you will learn the intricacies of small claims court. Classes such as these can also teach you how to write a living will or a contract, create a trust, plan your estate, or aid one of your relatives. Even if you don't learn all the details of how to write and create legal documents yourself, you will become familiar with their execution and know what to look for in the legal documents of others for your protection. Law-related classes can also help with purchasing real estate and insurance. Even if you're not really interested in law, classes such as these are helpful in real life situations. Although you may engage a professional to assist you with legal matters, such as trust funds, real estate purchases, or your will, it helps to be familiar with what they do. And, these classes can be highly interesting.

Some quick tips for getting the most out of *all* your classes:

- Sit in the front or middle of the classroom. This will improve your grades for two reasons. You'll pay more attention if the professor is constantly staring you in the face or standing in front of you to make his point. From the professor's perspective, he will probably notice you more and appreciate the fact that you are listening. This could earn you more consideration when class participation and attitude factor are figured into your borderline grade of B but an *nth* away from an A, or a D but an *nth* away from a C. Get the picture? The professor may also be willing to devote more of his office hours to help you understand a difficult concept.

- Visit your professors' offices often, when class first starts and when finals are approaching. Most students who are lackadaisical about the class, sit in the back and chat, or don't go and then show up the week before finals to beg the professor for lenience in her grading policy or for extra help in understanding something it took her weeks to explain, may receive less than full concern.

- Get to class on time. Show interest in the lecture. Follow the discussion. This is not only respectful, it also keeps you in your professor's favor, or at least out of his disfavor.

- Participate! Participate! Participate!

- Ask questions. You'll never learn if you don't ask questions about concepts you don't understand. Even if you think your question is stupid, the real stupidity is if you don't ask it and then whatever you didn't understand and didn't ask about appears on a test and you are unable to answer the question.

- Lend your own experience to the class discussions, by telling the class and professor about your internship at a manufacturing plant and how the term "bottleneck" applies to both the classroom discussion and the problem you had at the plant. It will help you to remember important points if you can relate them to your experiences. It also helps your professor place your name with your face if you contribute to discussions.

- Take notes and date them. It helps you when preparing for midterms, finals, or quizzes.

College is an exercise in mind control and discipline. Even though a class may seem exceedingly boring and without real-life application, it's not so. College is life. College is aerobics and jazzercise for the mind. You will use your mind every day for the rest of your life. You might as well whip it into shape while you're in college.

STUDENT HIGHLIGHT

David Buckholtz, a sophomore at Emory University, really enjoyed his reading and writing journals course. Instead of participating in classroom discussions about people and places or discussing literary works, David and his classmates were encouraged to explore their personal histories and origins and record their observations in a journal. The class revolved around external learning factors rather than internal classroom factors such as textbooks or the professor. David explains: "As opposed to a traditional English course, we didn't just read books about places, we actually went there and met the people we read about. For the course, I traveled the Georgia barrier islands extensively as well as other parts of Southern Georgia such as the Okefenokee swamp. My final project for the class was to travel back to Warner Robins, Georgia, with my grandmother and write down my history and connection with Georgia in a journal. Warner Robins is where my mother grew up and where my grandmother spent thirty years of her life. I researched many places around Georgia to get a historical balance to my families' experiences." David feels that his experience with this class has been unforgettable, particularly in his personal development.

UNIVERSITY HIGHLIGHTS
MANAGEMENT 101 AT BUCKNELL UNIVERSITY

Firsthand experience in management is the name of the game for business management students at Bucknell University in Lewisburg, Pennsylvania. Management 101 is a course in which students run their own temporary companies and donate any earnings they accumulate to charity.

According to Professor Tammy Hiller, at the beginning of the semester, students submit business plans with their ideas. Once the business plan is approved, a loan is issued by the Management (MG101) Corporation. The MG101 corporation's board of directors, made up of Professor John Miller, who initiated the program in 1978, Professor Tammy Hiller, student teaching assistants, and other management faculty, then issues a loan to the student company, ranging from $500 to $5,000 depending on the nature of the business plan.

Past student companies include a nightclub, now called the Terrace Room, and still in existence for special events, a T-shirt business, and a beach towel venture. One of the most imaginative companies was Campus Sounds, a company formed to produce and distribute a compact disc of local campus bands.

During the semester approximately four companies operate simultaneously. The companies are usually run by thirty students or fewer and generally make a profit of $1,000 per semester. Past donations to charity have gone to local headstarts for renovating playgrounds, elderly groups for giving parties, and local environmental groups for clean up campaigns.

EXPERIENCE THE GREAT OUTDOORS WITH COURSES AT ST. LAWRENCE UNIVERSITY

St. Lawrence University in Canton, New York, encourages its students to experience the great outdoors firsthand with its Outdoor Education Program. The program combines hiking, canoeing, or rafting with courses on the environment.

THE PROFESSOR

As you have already learned, professors can be an extremely valuable source of information and advice. These individuals, although paid, have basically devoted at least a portion of their lives to helping you get an education. If you think about it, at no other point in your life will you find such a concentrated cluster of professionals, specialists, scholars, researchers, and champions. At Florida A & M there is a slew of lawyers, accountants, doctors, corporate executives, authors, researchers, scientists, investment analysts, marketing managers, real estate and insurance agents, and once even a chess champion.

Most professors are a valuable source of information both inside and outside of the classroom. During class, you may learn what's in the textbooks (which by the way, are mostly written by professors). After class, you can learn more about topics covered in the course that can help you tremendously in other areas of your life. Some professors regularly throw out information they think you might need. The professor of my commercial law class, Ronald Jarrett, interspersed his regular lectures with information on tax laws, how to help your parents establish a trust for you, how to write your will, why you need renter's insurance, how to set up your own business, and how to buy real estate. The knowledge that I and many of my classmates gained from courses like accounting, investments, commercial law, the legal environment of business, and marketing management have helped us in a number of situations.

Many of the professors will offer their professional services for free either during or after office hours. There were several professors on my campus who offered legal services and conducted seminars free of charge. This sort of advice can have numerous uses in sticky situations. For instance, think about roommates. Roommates can be great! They are friends, cramming buddies, and someone with whom to share expenses and household chores. On the other hand, roommates can steal, lie, run up the phone bill, and check out on a joint rental lease, leaving you holding the bag. Students left in such a situation, already having little or no cash flow, sought the advice of the professors on campus who were willing to help. This usually resulted in a happy ending—the wronged roommate received compensation without paying expensive legal fees.

Professors and instructors help in other ways, too. As a first-semester junior, I wrote a paper for an organizational behavior class. I entitled the paper "Knowledge Creation Within a Company." When my professor for the class, George Neely, returned my paper, I saw not only an A, but also his handwritten, "Come see me!" under my grade. Fearing accusations of plagiarism and collaboration and carefully building a case to prove otherwise, I finally visited his office after several weeks of deliberation. He asked me if I had ever thought about graduate school. I said yes. He then explained several facts and ideas about graduate school, including its importance. He also recommended a program on campus that specialized in preparing students for graduate school and helped the students in the program to find summer research assignments. Even better, before I left his office, he called the director of the McNair Scholars Program and referred me to him.

Professors and instructors are excellent sources for advice and consultations. They can also be wonderful mentors. All you need do is ask. They may say "No," but more often you'll hear "Yes, I'll help."

YOUR CLASS SCHEDULE AND YOUR GPA

As you begin your college career—or even if you're in the middle of it—I'm sure you have thought about your grade point average (GPA). When I started college I didn't really worry about it, but as sophomore year rolled around, the all-important grade factor began to occupy more and more of my thoughts. Although I am a strong proponent of overall learning and life outside the classroom, I am also an advocate of maintaining a life inside the classroom. It should always be one of your goals to maximize your chance to have an outstanding transcript, as well as have fun and take interesting courses in the process of getting it. Let me explain what I did to fulfill this.

I developed a master plan during my sophomore year that allowed me to make good grades and enjoy myself, especially as a senior, even though I knew I would also be concentrating on admission to graduate school, getting a job, or both. Referencing our course curriculum in the college catalog for my school and major, I listed all of the classes I was required to take. I totaled the number of hours required for graduation as a business administration major. I listed the courses and hours I had already taken and compared them to the requirements and plotted my course from that point. I realized that the more hours I took toward graduation requirements as an underclassman (freshman and sophomore years) the more I would be able to relax as an upperclassman. For me, relaxation meant learning about something I've always been interested in rather than getting heavily involved and never surfacing from business school and the world of facts, figures, balance sheets, and the all-important bottom line. I called classes I chose enhancement classes. Also, I wanted my last days of college to be laid-back, as far as graduation was concerned. Even though I knew other important activities would be occupying my time—searching for a job, applying to graduate school, and applying for fellowships—I realized quickly that getting required classes out of the way left the field clear for me to focus on the rest of my life. So I budgeted my time. I knew that to achieve my goal of getting graduation requirements out of the way before senior year, I needed to take at least 36 hours per year, 18 hours per semester. Even though it was at times grueling, by the beginning of my junior year, I was able to decrease my hours to 16, then finally 14. In my senior year, I took piano lessons (something I had always wanted to do), psychology (another developing interest), golf, Spanish, and several other elective courses.

Maintaining your grades from the time you enter college is important not only for purposes of relaxation, reduced stress, and taking enhancement classes. When you are applying for jobs or graduate school, your transcript is not going to reflect your final GPA. It will only reflect your grades from the past semester. So unless you are planning to postpone your job or graduate school search until well after you have graduated, you should make sure your grades are up to par before your senior year so you won't be scrambling to bolster your GPA and your ego as admissions officials and recruiters tell you they're not interested.

To have fun and get good grades, plan your schedule wisely. Know the grades you need to make to achieve the GPA you want. Then go to work! In the words of Zig Ziglar, motivational speaker and chairman of the Zig Ziglar Corporation, "You don't pay the price for hard work, you enjoy the benefits. Life is tough, but if you're tough on life, life will be infinitely easier. When you do the things you ought to do when you ought to do them, the day will come when you can do the things you want to do when you want to do them."

5

LEARNING BEYOND THE CLASSROOM

Have you ever wanted to visit another part of the country, meet new people, escape from the humdrum of the classroom, or earn a few extra dollars working in a field that interests you? If you answered yes to any of those questions, then an applied learning program is definitely the route for you. Applied learning, an educational tool that has been in existence for over half a century, can be found in several different forms. It includes cooperative education (co-ops), internships, experiential learning, apprenticeships, and occupational learning. These are all based on experience and learning that occurs almost entirely beyond the classroom. Applied learning also allows self-assessment, the clarification of goals, and the identification of entry barriers within a particular field.

The benefits of applied learning are recognized at most post-secondary institutions. The University of Cincinnati was one of the first institutions to use applied learning as an educational tool, followed by Antioch University, Georgia Institute of Technology, and Drexel University. Currently, almost every post-secondary institution has some form of or access to applied learning programs. Let's consider some of the benefits of applied learning.

Benefits

- Work experience—An internship, co-op, or other form of applied learning can provide you with actual work experience in the field in which you are interested. When you participate in an internship a potential employer can assess your work habits to see if they will fit within that organization. In turn, you can assess yourself to decide if you actually want to work in that particular field.

- Money—Many internships and cooperative programs are paid. Some companies and organizations may take care of living expenses as well. Corporate internships usually pay approximately 75 to 80 percent of the monthly salary paid to full-time employees in a particular field. Nonprofit and government organizations usually pay considerably less than their corporate counterparts and may pay nothing. Your compensation will depend on the organization, your field of interest, and the location of the internship. Regardless of whether the internship does or does not pay, it is a valuable source of work experience and may also have many of the other benefits listed here.

- Contacts—As you get to know individuals within an organization you begin to develop contacts. You can refer to your contacts in the future to gain job-related or other types of information. For example, John Doe at XYZ company may keep you in mind or know of a job opening at XYZ that would be perfect for you when you graduate. When I was an intern at EDS in Belgium, I needed some information from a written document that I had completed the previous year at EDS in Raleigh, North Carolina. I called one of my contacts at the Raleigh office and she sent that document overnight, as well as others that were helpful.

- References—In many applied learning programs you may have several supervisors and can use other coworkers as mentors. These individuals can serve as excellent references since they have firsthand knowledge of your abilities.

These references can be used not only for employment purposes but also when applying for graduate school, scholarships, fellowships, and merit awards.

- Travel—Some internships and co-op programs offer opportunities to travel. For example, as a sales intern for Armstrong, I went to New York, New Jersey, Baltimore, and Washington. Travel opportunities will depend on the organization, the job itself, and the primary location of the internship.

- Mentors—Many prominent and successful men and women have attributed at least part of their success to the presence of a mentor in their lives. Mentors are people who can see the promise in a young individual, especially one in their career field. As a mentor they take the time to steer that individual in the right direction, give insight into a particular field, and offer tips on avoiding standard pitfalls. Essentially, they aid others by relating the knowledge that they have gained through life in general and through working for a number of years in a particular career. Internships and co-ops are excellent opportunities to find and develop lasting relationships with people who can help shape your life and career.

- Technical skills—As an intern or co-op, you may be taught certain skills in workshops, training sessions, or seminars in order to do your job effectively. These skills may be particular to an industry or they may be applicable to other jobs or activities you decide to undertake. For example, in my first internship with EDS in Raleigh, North Carolina, I learned the difference between technical writing and creative writing. I also learned how to use MacDraw and Microsoft Word software applications on Macintosh computers and operating systems. In addition, we worked entirely in teams, and at the end of my internship I functioned as a manager of one of the teams. During my internship with Armstrong World Industries, interns participated in several seminars on topics including selling skills, goal setting, presentation skills, relationship strategies, and writing skills. All of these seminars contributed significantly to my development as an individual, but all are relevant to any job or activity, not just an Armstrong marketing representative. In sum, I developed the following skills from my internship: technical writing, managing and working with the team-based approach, and computer skills and proficiency with MacDraw and Microsoft Word on a new (to me) but widely used hardware system. I also acquired other, less obvious skills such as effective time management because we worked under deadline almost entirely, as well as how to manage stress in our deadline-oriented environment.

- Enhanced knowledge through application—Application of the knowledge you gain in class can solidify and enhance what you have learned. For example, I did not fully understand the concepts in my production management class. Even though I did well, just-in-time management and other expediting functions were memory definitions for me, not actual applications. However, because of my internship with Armstrong, I understand not only the definitions but also how these concepts might be needed in the business world. In addition, I was able to present my own examples in class for discussion purposes.

- Decision tool—Your internship or other applied learning experience is always a decision tool. Even if you are interning in a field totally unrelated to your major, the internship can help you decide whether you like that field enough to abandon your current major and try another, whether you want to double major, or whether you want to develop this new interest into a minor. When making a career choice later, your internship or applied learning experience will also aid you in making difficult choices, including multiple job offers, graduate school admissions, or fellowships.

- Possible job offer after graduation—Although for most it is a possibility and not a guarantee, if you do an excellent job as an intern or co-op, you have a good chance of being offered a job after you graduate. The company gains by having much of your training already done when you were an intern or co-op; you gain by having a possible job offer in your back pocket.

- Books—Books are sometimes given to interns to further their development in a particular area. These books may be especially helpful for research in a later required class.
- Scholarship aid—Some companies and organizations that sponsor internships offer scholarships to those who are selected to participate.
- Friends—During your internship or co-op program you will probably hang out with other interns, co-ops, or employees at the company or organization in which you work. In the midst of the fun, laughter, and work some of these may become lasting friendships. These friends could become valuable contacts for you in the future, particularly if they work for the organization in which you interned or for another organization that also interests you.

EXPERIENTIAL OR OCCUPATIONAL LEARNING

Experiential or occupational learning is learning based on experience. Someone who has learned experientially or occupationally has already started his or her career or spent considerable time working in a particular area. For example, if you have worked for several years as a sales representative and then decide to go back to college to complete your degree in marketing, you may be eligible for academic credit for the years you spent on the job, depending on the college. The credit would be based on your past experiences and the knowledge you gained in your occupation. In some cases, internships and other applied learning programs are also considered experiential learning and are available for credit.

INTERNSHIPS

Internships are valuable experiences for all college students, for those who may need a little direction in deciding on a career as well as for those who hope to get a job in the current tight job market. Internships can be structured or unstructured forms of applied learning. They can be paid or unpaid. Internships can coincide with your academic program of study or be in another area, and can last from one month to several months. They are available in a range of organizations and locations. For example, an internship can be in a corporation, a medical laboratory, a newspaper, a department store, or on an archaeological site. Through an internship you can strengthen your knowledge base and also determine whether your major and field of interest are right for you. An internship can result in your meeting people who could be extremely helpful and resourceful contacts for you in the future, and it allows you to apply the knowledge that you have learned from textbooks and professors to the real world. An internship is also a good start in making the transition from insulated college life to the hectic environment beyond the college campus. It may involve travel all over the United States or even the world.

Before my internship with Armstrong World Industries, a manufacturing company based in Lancaster, Pennsylvania, I knew nothing of the sales and marketing field. Previously, the idea of selling anyone anything was extremely distasteful to me. When I read Armstrong's job description for a summer internship as a marketing representative, my mind focused on two words, "sales territory," immediately conjuring up images of selling doughnuts, candy, and other knickknacks for numerous school projects and clubs as a child. I remembered the horrors of having people give me the sweet and often false response "We already have" to my childish sales pitch "Would you like to buy some of our. . . ." I also remembered our house being filled with merchandise that my mother bought to keep me from suffering repeated rejections and further injury to my pint-sized ego. Needless to say, a sales internship did not appeal to me. However, because I liked the company overall and especially the recruiters, I decided to give it a try. It was one of the best decisions I have ever made—I discovered I love sales and marketing! My childhood fears have been replaced by an adult reality. Had I never experienced the Armstrong sales internship, my career options would have been limited, mainly due to my own ignorance. Now I know that the field of sales and marketing is highly interesting, charged with responsibility, and can be extremely profitable. Not only that, most jobs in this field are consulting oriented, rather than make-the-sale-no-matter-what oriented. Through this experience I learned that if a customer has a need or a problem and you as the sales representative demonstrate the knowledge, experience, and willingness to satisfy his or her needs while providing an effective solution for the problem, the sale will follow. Until my internship with Armstrong, I never knew that. Since that summer, I have developed a fascination with this field and have even taken courses to further my interest.

For most college graduates relevant work experience is a necessity for landing at least one job offer. In the 90s most employers want to see students who not only have good GPAs, but also potential. They want students who can walk into a job and hit the ground running. Because most companies are right-sizing, streamlining, and downsizing, students are under increasing pressure to show their talents and value to potential employers. One of the best ways to do so is to have had at least one internship in the field you plan to enter. But internships can only be valuable in this way if you know how to sell the experience you have gained from them and show your resulting growth as an individual. If you have had an internship, highlight the job duties and responsibilities it carried on your résumé in the work experience section as shown in the résumés in chapter 2. You also need to be prepared to emphasize your internship during interviews with potential employers. If it's on your résumé, they will probably ask about it. When you talk about the internship, be certain to show confidence and assert the effort and knowledge that you contributed and gained from the internship.

Many career centers at universities and colleges can help students find internships with major corporations, public service agencies, the government, or other profit or nonprofit entities. Some also sponsor internship expositions which hundreds of these organizations participate in.

Remember, the very least an internship can do is give you some work experience. In today's job society that is what matters most. Use your time at college wisely and get the most for your money by holding at least one internship. You may find that it will change your life. You can learn more about internship opportunities by visiting the career center or placement office at your college or university, by referring to the books and magazines listed below, or by writing directly to the organizations at the addresses provided.

Publications

The Congressional Intern Handbook
Congressional Management Foundation
513 Capitol Court, NW,
Suite 100
Washington, DC 20002

Directory of Internships
Ready Reference Press
PO Box 5249
Santa Monica, CA 90409

Directory of Special Programs for Minority Group Members: Career Information Services, Employment Skills, Banks, Financial Aid Sources
by Willis L. Johnson
Garrett Park Press
PO Box 190 C
Garrett Park, MD 20896-0190

*Directory of Student
  Placements in Health Care
  Settings in North America*
Association for the Care of
  Children's Health
7910 Woodmont Avenue,
Suite 300
Bethesda, MD 20814

A *Directory of Washington,
  DC, Internships*
University Resource Services
PO Box 3722
Stanford, CA 94309

*The Experienced Hand: A
  Student Manual for Making
  The Most of an Internship*
by Timothy Stanton
and Kamil Ali
Carrol Press
43 Squantum Street
Cranston, RI 02920

Peterson's Internships 1996
Peterson's Guides, Inc.
PO Box 2123
Princeton, NJ 08543-2123

*San Francisco Bay Area and
  Silicon Valley Internship
  Directory*
University Resource Services
PO Box 3722
Stanford, CA 94309

*Storming Washington: An
  Intern's Guide to National
  Government*
American Political Science
  Association

1527 New Hampshire
  Avenue, NW
Washington, DC 20036

*Student Guide to Mass Market
  Internships*
Intern Research Group
Department of Journalism
Southwest Texas State
University
San Marcos, TX 78666

The College Edition of the
  *National Business
  Employment Weekly,
  Managing Your Career*,
  published by *The Wall
  Street Journal*
Dow Jones & Company, Inc.
Headquarters
420 Lexington Ave.
NY, NY 10170

Job Choices published by the
  College Placement Council
College Placement
  Council, Inc.
620 Highland Avenue
Bethlehem, PA 18017

The Black Collegian published
  by Black Collegiate
  Services, Inc.
140 Carondelet Street
New Orleans, LA 70130

A Sampling of Companies and Organizations with Internship Programs

Abbot Laboratories
Manager, College Relations
One Abbot Park Road
Abbott Park, IL 60064

ADP
Human Resources
One ADP Boulevard
Roseland, NJ 07068

AETNA
Corporate College Relations
151 Farmington Avenue,
    Dept. 6017
Hartford, CT 06156

Apple Computer, Inc.
College Relations Department
20525 Mariani Avenue,
    MS 9ACR
Cupertino, CA 95014

AT&T
College Recruiting Manager
100 Southgate, 1st Floor
Morristown, NJ 07980-6441

Boeing, Inc.
PO Box 3707
7755 East Marginal Way S.
Seattle, WA 98124

BP America/BP Oil Recruiting
200 Public Square 11-B
Cleveland, Ohio 44115

Central Intelligence Agency
CIA Employment Center
PO Box 12727, Dept. 25AC
Arlington, VA 22209-8727

Dell Computer Corporation
University Relations
    Department
9505 Arboretum Boulevard
Austin, TX 78759

Eastman Kodak Company
Professional Staffing and
    University Development
943 State Street
Rochester, NY 14650-1139

The Electronics Boutique
College Recruitment
    Coordinator
1345 Enterprise Drive
West Chester, PA 19380

GE Recruiting & Technical
    Entry Programs
3135 Easton Turnpike
Dept. CPC
Fairfield, CT 06431

Hallmark Cards, Inc.
Manager, College Relations
2501 McGee
PO Box 419580
Kansas City, MO 64141-6580

Intel Corporation
3065 Bowers Avenue
Santa Clara, CA 95052

ITT Hartford
College Relations Program
 Manager
Hartford Plaza
Hartford, CT 06115

Lechters, Inc.
College Relations Department
1 Cape May Street
Harrison, NJ 07029

Link: The College Magazine
110 Green Street, Suite 407
New York, NY 10012
(212) 966-1100

Lucasfilm Ltd.
5858 Lucas Valley Road
Nicasio, CA 94946

McDonald's Corporation
Employment Consultant
Kroc Drive
Oak Brook, IL 60501

Merck & Co.
Office of College Relations
One Merck Drive
PO Box 100
Whitehouse Station, NJ 08889

Nine West Group
Attn.: Recruitment
9 West Broad Street
Stamford, CT 06902

SmithKline Beecham
US College Relations
200 North 16th Street
Philadelphia, PA 19101

Sony Electronics, Inc.
University Relations Manager
1 Sony Drive
Park Ridge, NJ 07656-8003

TBWA Advertising
292 Madison Avenue
New York, NY 10018

Union Pacific Technologies
Human Resources
7930 Calyton Road
St. Louis, MO 63117-1368

Washington Post
1150 15th St. NW
Washington, DC 20071

Washington Times
Manager, Human Resources
3600 New York Avenue, NE
Washington, DC 20071

WordPerfect Corporation
1555 North Technology Way,
 MS Q1311
Orem, UT 84057-2399

COOPERATIVE EDUCATION

Cooperative education combines formal academic training with actual work experience—either part-time or full-time work for which a student is usually paid—in a structured course of study. This type of program can last from several months to a year. Any of the following plans may be used for cooperative education (co-ops).

- Parallel—part-time work and part-time study
- Extended day—full-time study and part-time work or full-time work and part-time study
- Alternating—full-time work and full-time study in alternating patterns—for example, you can work one semester or quarter and study in school for the next semester or quarter.

Part-time study is a course load of less than 12 hours per semester or less than 9 hours per quarter.

STUDENT HIGHLIGHT

Applied learning in the form of cooperative education is a major decision tool and a very good source of both money and technical skills for Jany Kay Allen, a student at the Georgia Institute of Technology in Atlanta. Jany is involved in a cooperative education program with GDS, a small engineering consulting firm in Atlanta. She began the program as a sophomore in the fall of 1993 and completed it in the spring of 1996. (Georgia Tech requires students to work at least six quarters with a company.) During her co-op term, Jany has been involved in several in-house training programs, one of which helped to hone her technical writing skills, a key advantage in the consulting industry. She also says she is "very knowledgeable about several software programs which have definitely helped me in school." She also examined her company's affirmative action policies in a critical analysis speech prepared for a public speaking class. Jany explains: "Currently, GDS is not affected by affirmative action policies. As a result, we have only two professional women, no African Americans and no other minority groups on our payroll. I gave my speech as if I were talking to my company at an employee meeting."

For Jany, one of the biggest advantages from her co-op experience is the salary, which helps tremendously with tuition costs. Although her experience with GDS hasn't been all roses, her co-op experience *has* given her a good idea of how to approach future employment. Jany states, "I have enjoyed my co-op experience very much, but I know that I do not want to work for a small company now because I see a tremendous value in wellness programs, company outings, and team building. I do believe I will stay with consulting."

Cooperative Education Opportunities— Associations and Organizations

The Cooperative Education
  Association
8640 Guilford Road, Suite 215
Columbia, Maryland 21046
  (410) 290-3666

The National Commission for
  Cooperative Education
501 Stearns Center
360 Huntington Avenue
Boston, Massachusetts 02115
  (617) 373-5775

The Institute for Experimental
  Learning
1735 I Street, NW, Suite 716
Washington, DC 20006
  (202) 833-8580

The National Society for
  Experiential Education
3509 Haworth Drive, Suite 207
Raleigh, North Carolina 27609-
  7229   (919) 787-3263

The World Association for
  Cooperative Education
International Secretariat
c/o Mohawk College
PO Box 2034
Hamilton, Ontario, Canada
L8N 3T2   (416) 575-2296

A Sampling of Companies and Organizations
with Cooperative Education Programs

AETNA
Corporate College Relations
151 Farmington Avenue,
  Dept. 6017
Hartford, CT 06156

American International
  Group, Inc.
Manager, College Relations
72 Wall Street, 6th Floor
New York, NY 10270

AT&T
College Recruiting Manager
100 Southgate, 1st Floor
Morristown, NJ 07980-6441

BDO Seidman
Recruiting Director
15 Columbus Circle
New York, NY 10023

Board of Governors of the
  Federal Reserve System
Director of Human Resources
  Management

20th and Constitution
  Avenue, NW
Washington, DC 20551

Bonneville Power
  Administration
Recruiter
PO Box 3621
Portland, OR 97208

Central Intelligence Agency
CIA Employment Center
PO Box 12727, Dept. 25AC
Arlington, VA 22209-8727

Eastman Kodak Company
Professional Staffing and
  University Development
943 State Street
Rochester, NY 14650-1139

Electronic Data Systems
  Corporation
Staffing and Human Resources
5400 Legacy Drive
MS: H4-GB-35, Dept. 2214
Plano, TX 75024

Internal Revenue Service–U. S.
   Department of the Treasury
Cooperative Education
   Program Director
1111 Constitution
   Avenue, NW
Washington, DC 20004

Kellogg Company
College Recruitment
One Kellogg Square
PO Box 3599
Battle Creek, MI 49016-3599

Lechters, Inc.
College Relations
   Department
1 Cape May Street
Harrison, NJ 07029

LTV Steel Company
Manager, Human Resources
Personnel Department
PO Box 6778
Cleveland, OH 44101

MCI
Corporate College Relations
   Coordinator
1801 Pennsylvania Avenue, NW
Washington, DC 20006

Merck & Co.
Office of College Relations
One Merck Drive
PO Box 100
Whitehouse Station, NJ 08889

Nine West Group
Attn.: Recruitment
9 West Broad Street
Stamford, CT 06902

Phillips Petroleum Company
   and Subsidiaries
Manager, College and
   Employment Relations
180 Plaza Office Building
Bartlesville, OK 74004

SmithKline Beecham
US College Relations
200 North 16th Street
Philadelphia, PA 19101

Sony Electronics, Inc.
University Relations Manager
1 Sony Drive
Park Ridge, NJ 07656-8003

Toys "R" Us
HR Planning
461 From Road
Paramus, NJ 07652

U. S. Army Corps of Engineers
Directorate of Human
   Resources
20 Massachusetts Ave, NW
Washington, DC 20314-1000

U.S. Department of Labor
200 Constitution Avenue, NW
Dept. CP, Room S1002
Washington, DC 20210

SUMMER JOBS/PROGRAMS

Some corporations offer jobs to college students for the summer only. Internships and summer jobs are similar. The major difference between a summer job and an internship is that almost all summer jobs are paid positions, whereas many internships are not. In addition, internships can occur at any time during the school year, rather than just in the summer, as long as it is agreed upon by you and the organization or corporation for which you will be working. Also, most internships are structured programs designed to provide the most beneficial learning experience possible for you as the intern and also for the corporation, should they decide to hire to you for a permanent job. Lastly, for many internships you can get academic credit, whereas for most summer jobs you cannot. However, a summer job can still be a tremendous learning experience and it carries many of the same benefits as those outlined for internships and co-ops. In some cases, you may be able to get a summer job transferred into an internship and receive academic credit for it. Consult someone in your major department or the career center first to learn whether this is an option.

The following organizations offer summer opportunities to college students.

Publications

Seasonal Employment
National Park Service
Department of the Interior
Box 37127
Washington, DC 20013
  (202) 208-6985

Summer Employment Directory of The United States
Peterson's Guides, Inc.
PO Box 2123
Princeton, NJ 08543-2123
  (609) 243-9111

*Summer Opportunities in
Marine and Environmental
Science: A Student's Guide to
Jobs, Internships and Study,
Camp and Travel Programs*
Summer Opportunities Guide
38 Litchfield Road
Londonderry, NH 03053

Summer Jobs
U.S. Department of Trans-
portation/U. S. Coast Guard
2100 2nd Street, SW
Washington, DC 20593

*Summer Jobs: Opportunities in
the Federal Government*
Office of Personnel
Management
1900 E Street, NW
Washington, DC
20415   (202) 606-2424

*Summer Jobs USA: Where The
Jobs Are and How To Get
Them '96* (updated annually)
Peterson's Guides, Inc.
PO Box 2123
Princeton, NJ 08543-2123
(609) 243-9111

A Sampling of Summer Job Opportunities

AETNA
Corporate College Relations
151 Farmington Avenue,
    Dept. 6017
Hartford, CT 06156

American Frozen Foods, Inc.
National Recruitment Office
355 Benton Street
Stratford, CT 06497
    (800)233-5554

American International
    Group, Inc.
Manager, College Relations
72 Wall Street, 6th Floor
New York, NY 10270

AT&T
College Recruiting Manager
100 Southgate, 1st Floor
Morristown, NJ 07980-6441

BDO Seidman
Recruiting Director
15 Columbus Circle
New York, NY 10023

Board of Governors of The
    Federal Reserve System
Director of Human Resources
    Management
20th and Constitution
    Avenue, NW
Washington, DC 20551

Bonneville Power
    Administration
Recruiter
PO Box 3621
Portland, OR 97208

The Clorox Company
Senior College Relations
  Specialist
PO Box 24305
Oakland, CA 94623

Commodity Futures Trading
  Commission
Office of Personnel
2033 K Street, NW
Washington, DC 20581

Deloitte & Touche
Manager, Recruiting & College
  Relations
Ten Westport Road
PO Box 820
Wilton, CT 06897-0820

Discover Card Services
Human Resources Department
2500 Lake Cook Road
Riverwoods, IL 60015

Eastman Kodak Company
Professional Staffing and
  University Development
943 State Street
Rochester, NY 14650-1139

Electronic Data Systems
  Corporation
Staffing and Human Resources
5400 Legacy Drive
MS: H4-GB-35, Dept. 2214
Plano, TX 75024

Enterprise Rent-A-Car
National Headquarters
Personnel Manager
8850 Ladue Road
St. Louis, MO 63124

Famous Footwear
Recruitment and Training
  Manager
208 E. Olin Avenue
Madison, WI 53713

Hallmark Cards, Inc.
Manager, College Relations
2501 McGee
PO Box 419580
Kansas City, MO 64141-6580

Haworth
College Relations
One Haworth Center
Holland, MI 49423

IBP, Inc.
College Relations
  Representative
PO Box 8000
Sioux City, IA 55102

Kellogg Company
College Recruitment
One Kellogg Square
PO Box 3599
Battle Creek, MI 49016-3599

Lechters, Inc.
College Relations Department
1 Cape May Street
Harrison, NJ 07029

LTV Steel Company
Manager, Human Resources
Personnel Department
PO Box 6778
Cleveland, OH 44101

MCI
Corporate College Relations
    Coordinator
1801 Pennsylvania Avenue, NW
Washington, DC 20006

Merck & Co.
Office of College Relations
One Merck Drive
PO Box 100
Whitehouse Station, NJ 08889

National Credit Union
    Administration
Office of Human Resources
1775 Duke Street
Alexandria, VA 22314-3428

National Security Agency
Attention: M3221 (AGU)
Fort George G. Meade, MD
    20755-6000

NIH Employment Office
Summer Program Coordinator
Building 31, Room B3C15
9000 Rockville Pike
Bethesda, MD 20892
    (301) 496-2403

Northern Illinois Gas
Recruiting Administrator
PO Box 190
Aurora, IL 60507

Phillips Petroleum Company
    and Subsidiaries
Manager, College and
    Employment Relations
180 Plaza Office Building
Bartlesville, OK 74004

Pizza Hut, Inc.
College Relations Manager
9111 East Douglas
Wichita, KS 67207

The Sherwin Williams
    Company
Director of Personnel
101 Prospect Avenue
Cleveland, OH 44115

SmithKline Beecham
US College Relations
200 North 16th Street
Philadelphia, PA 19101

Toys "R" Us
HR Planning
461 From Road
Paramus, NJ 07652

Union Pacific Technologies
Human Resources
7930 Calyton Road
St. Louis, MO 63117-1368

U. S. Army Corps of Engineers
Directorate of Human
    Resources
20 Massachusetts Ave, NW
Washington, DC 20314-1000

Whirlpool Corporation
Corporate Recruiting
2000 M-63, MAILDROP
  2900 CPC
Benton Harbor, MI 49022

RESEARCH PROGRAMS

If you really want to explore your major and all of its possibilities, getting involved in a research program is an excellent way to do so. Most research programs are structured to allow you to conduct your research independently, as part of a team, or with a professor or other faculty member. Research programs allow you to delve deeper into a particular field. You might even uncover incredible information. For example, as part of a research effort, several math majors at Florida A & M University constructed mathematical models as a solution to cancer. Who would think of math as a solution for helping to find a cure for a disease? If you get involved in a research program, you might think of math, science, sociology, or statistics in a variety of different ways that only a serious researcher would know about. For students interested in a summer research program, AT&T Bell Laboratories offers a program for minorities and women at their research and development laboratories in New Jersey and Pennsylvania. The program is designed to attract students into scientific careers by placing participants in working contact with experienced research scientists and engineers. For more information, contact Special Programs Manager-SRP, University Relations Center, 600 Mountain Avenue, Room 3D-304, Murray Hill, NJ 07974-0636.

STUDENT HIGHLIGHT

Angela Grant, a Ph.D. candidate at the University of Michigan, believes that her research experience at the University of Illinois in Champaign was one of the key factors in her acceptance in the graduate program and her winning a prestigious National Science Foundation Fellowship. Angela had taken advantage of a summer research opportunity program during her undergraduate college career. Not only did she have an interest-ing summer exploring the vast world of pure mathematics at its best and worst, but her research experience also helped to propel her toward earning her doctorate in math.

DIRECTED INDIVIDUAL STUDY (DIS)

Directed individual study is academic course work usually supervised by an advisor from your department. You may design the course under the supervision of your advisor, and decide your own pace. In many cases, the advisor may administer tests or require a written paper, presentation, research project, or all three upon completion of your studies. The period of study usually lasts the length of a regular class term. You won't have classes to attend, but you may have periodic meetings with your advisor to discuss your progress. For DIS you could receive anywhere from one to six credit hours, possibly more. Credit depends on your advisor, the department, and the quantity and quality of work you do. This program may not be available everywhere.

6

THE INTERNATIONAL EXPERIENCE

If you want to escape the traditional confines of your university or college and further your education and experience in an international setting, then working or studying abroad may be just the thing for you. To most graduate schools and prospective employers, global experience is a key factor in acceptance or getting the job. So have a little fun, experience a new culture, and enlighten your mind with the traditions and customs of a different country. Go abroad! Although you may have visited a foreign country before, living, working, or studying in one is a completely different experience.

A LITTLE ABOUT GOING ABROAD

Going to live and work abroad is an undertaking that requires careful planning. There are many books dedicated solely to the experience of working and studying abroad, so I will not go too deeply into the planning process. However, I will provide you with a little background information and tell you about my own experiences abroad.

Work and study abroad programs are sponsored by universities here in the United States and by a consortium of universities that have formed an independent organization for the specific purpose of fostering international student endeavors. Programs are also sponsored by independent organizations that have no ties to a specific university, college, or consortium in the United States.

The Council on International Educational Exchange (CIEE), with offices worldwide, is one of the largest and most comprehensive organizations currently offering assistance to students who wish to travel, work, or study abroad. CIEE has many divisions offering numerous services. For example, CIEE maintains the information and student services department, which issues the international student identity card and the youth international identity card for those under 26, and answers thousands of inquiries from students interested in going abroad. When I went to Brussels, Belgium, as an intern for Electronic Data Systems (EDS) in the summer of 1993, the company and its expatriate administration used the services of CIEE to obtain a work permit for me. The idea of a student travel card came from the International Student Travel Confederation, which is made up of student travel organizations in 74 countries. The card allows discounts at theaters, movies, museums, restaurants, train stations, and so on. In addition to these discounts and others related to travel, the card also provides basic accident and medical coverage, as well as a 24-hour emergency hotline. It is worth the minimal fee.

Before I went to Brussels, I also made use of the free student travel catalog published by CIEE. The catalog is a 76-page guide full of useful information including articles, forms to apply for the identity card, tips on what to bring, and a host of other information designed to help students make their travels a worthwhile and exhilarating experience. CIEE also publishes the comprehensive *Work Study, Travel Abroad: The Whole World Handbook*.

Council Travel is part of CIEE's travel services department, and offers the following:

- Budget airfares between the United States and Europe, Asia, the South Pacific, Africa, the Middle East, Latin America, and the Caribbean

- Rail passes, including Eurail, Britrail, and Frenchrail
- International student identity card
- Car rentals in Europe
- Language course in cities throughout Europe and Japan
- Travel insurance, guidebooks, and travel gear

I used or inquired about most of these services at one time or another while I prepared for my internship in Brussels. I found the airfares varied. Although my airfare was covered by EDS, the company I interned with, my best friend was planning to visit and needed the lowest possible airfare. I encouraged her to get a youth international identity card, as I had, so we could take advantage of special student discounts. We both shopped around for the best airfares. Even though we thought that airfares offered by Council Travel would be the least expensive, we actually found that a flight on Delta Airlines was the best, at $500 for a roundtrip ticket from Atlanta to Brussels. We later traveled with another friend to various cities throughout Europe. Although the Eurail passes offered by Council Travel were a great deal, all three of us found that, armed with the youth international ID card, we could get super train fares at the spur of the moment to any city. It was wonderful and—most important, from our college students' perspective—it was cheap!

For those wanting to travel with freedom, Council Charter, a subsidiary of CIEE, has chartered flights to various cities all over the world. Two of the great advantages of this service are that it allows you to fly into one city and return from another, and it offers low cost cancellation waivers.

OVERSEAS JOB OPPORTUNITIES

Students interested in working abroad must wade through mounds of red tape to be able to officially enter and work in another country. Organizations such as the Council on International Educational Exchange (CIEE) can help to sort out questions and problems and can aid a student in making a smooth transition between countries. For example, through CIEE, students can get information on employment authorization needed, such as a work permit, general information on the country, helpful tips on finding employment once they arrive, and housing and travel information. CIEE publishes a magazine containing most of this information. In many countries, CIEE maintains an office or has ties with a student organization that will sponsor you and provide general assistance once you arrive in the country. CIEE's work exchanges department handles inquiries of students interested in working abroad.

Inter-Exchange, a private, nonprofit organization, also helps U.S. citizens find short-term job and au pair (see below) opportunities throughout Western and Eastern Europe in countries including the Czech Republic, Hungary, Finland, France, Germany, Norway, and Switzerland. Job opportunities are in the areas of general farm work, teaching English, hotel maintenance, and so on. For more details, contact Inter-Exchange, 161 Sixth Avenue, New York, NY 10013, (212) 924-0446.

The following are several of the many different opportunities for working abroad.

The Au Pair

Would you like to stay in someone's home and be an au pair? Au pairs are usually young single women interested in learning the language and culture of a particular country. By arrangement, the student lives with and cares for the children of a host family. On my trip to Belgium, my seatmate on the airplane was a Belgian au pair returning from Los Angeles. She shared with me her views on our country and what she missed most about her own during her stay in America. She said she missed Belgian bread the most. Ours was too soft! Besides the bread, she told me she had improved her English a lot, and that she liked to go to the movie theater and to concerts. She also loved our libraries. Au pairs are expected to work from 30 to 45 hours per week caring for the children of the host family. This could include playing with the children, taking the children to and from school, or helping with their homework. If you are interested in becoming an au pair, contact Au Pair/Homestay Abroad, 1015 15th Street NW, Suite 750, Washington, DC 20005, (202) 408-5380. Opportunities currently exist in France, Germany, Great Britain, Iceland, Norway, Argentina, The Netherlands, and Switzerland. You can also contact the following organizations: Au Pair Intercultural, 741 S.W. Lincoln Street, Portland, OR 97201-3178, (800) 654-2051; American Institute for Foreign Study Au Pair Program, 102 Greenwich Avenue, Greenwich, CT 06830, (800) 727-2437.

International Internships

The International Association of Students in Economics and Commerce (AIESEC) offers full-time students at colleges and universities worldwide the opportunity to gain hands-on management and leadership skills with a global perspective. Students can participate in international conferences or work abroad in an internship exchange program in a variety of business-related fields. For more information, contact AIESEC, 841 Broadway, Suite 608, New York, NY 10003, (212) 979-7400.

Practical on-the-job experience for college and university students is one of the services offered by the International Association for the Exchange of Students for Technical Experience (IAESTE). Students of architecture, computer science, engineering, mathematics, and other related technical fields have the opportunity to gain experience in more than 50 countries. For further information, contact IAESTE Training Program, c/o Association for International Practical Training, 10 Corporate Center, 10400 Little Patuxent Parkway, Columbia, MD 21044-3510, (301) 997-2200.

The Overseas Development Network sponsors internships for its Social Justice Program. Interns are placed with a development organization in Latin America, India, the Philippines, or Zimbabwe. For more information, contact the Overseas Development Network, 333 Valencia Street, Suite 330, San Francisco, CA 94103.

People to People International is an organization that sponsors two-month unpaid professional internships to students primarily interested in international business or relations. Students who participate shadow and observe professionals in various positions. Some of the companies and organizations in which students have been placed in the past are the Royal Bank of Scotland, the London Chamber of Commerce and Industry, the Danish Red Cross, and the Geological Survey Office of Dublin, Ireland. Students can get six units of undergraduate or graduate credit for the internship. For more information, write to People to People International, 501 East Armour Boulevard, Kansas City, MO 64109, (816) 531-4701.

The YMCA of Washington, D.C., also has an internship program, the YMCA Intern Abroad, that allows students to work with YMCA staff members on various projects. For example, you could intern in Australia, the Bahamas, Austria, Bangladesh, France, England, Egypt, Ireland, or Kenya, among many other countries. Write to Washington DC Metro YMCA, 1625 Massachusetts Avenue, NW, Suite 700, Washington, DC 20036.

Other International Internship Opportunities

Educational Programs Abroad
3415 N. 15th Street
Arlington, VA 22201   (703) 522-6562

Internships International LLC
116 Cowper Drive
Raleigh, NC 27608
(919) 832-1575

Volunteer Abroad—Work Camps, Farming, Field Research

If you are interested in volunteering your services abroad, CIEE operates a voluntary service department that maintains an international program that allows interested students to participate in short-term programs. You could be placed in one of various countries throughout Europe, Africa, North America, or Asia to work on a project. You may also want to read *Volunteer! The Comprehensive Guide to Voluntary Service in the US and Abroad*, a guide to hundreds of volunteer opportunities throughout the United States and all over the world, published jointly by the Council on International Educational Exchange and Commission on Voluntary Service and Action (CVSA).

Work camps. Work camps are just what they sound like—camps where you work. Groups of people from all over the world are involved in a specific project at each camp. Projects are unique opportunities for individuals to make a significant difference in the countries in which they are situated. For example, projects range from educating youth to environmental conservation to restoration of a medieval castle to the actual building of school in an impoverished country.

Volunteers for Peace coordinates work camps in more than thirty-four countries. For more information, contact Volunteers for Peace, 43 Tiffany Road, Belmont, VT 05730, (802) 259-2759.

The World Council of Churches sponsors summer work camp programs in Africa, Asia, and the Middle East. Participants help construct schools, churches, or other community buildings. For more information write to Ecumenical Youth Action, World Council of Churches, 150 rue de Ferney, PO Box 2100, 1211 Geneva 2, Switzerland.

Other International Volunteer Programs

Community Service Volunteers
Overseas Programme
237 Pentonville Road
London
N1 9NJ England, UK   011-44-171-278-6601

SCI-International Voluntary Service
Route 2, Box 506
Crozet, VA 22932   (804) 823-1826

Volunteers in Service to America (VISTA)
1100 Vermont Avenue, NW, Suite 8100
Washington DC 20525   (800) 424-8867, (202) 606-4845

Farming. The WOOF (Working for Organic Growers) Organization was established to give people the opportunity to gain
experience in the field of organic farming and gardening in
exchange for volunteer work on a farm. For more information
on volunteering, contact, NEWOOF (Northeast Workers on
Organic Farms), c/o The New England Small Farm Institute,
PO Box 608, Belchertown, MA 01007, (413) 323-4531.

Field research. Volunteers work with scientists on field research
projects in countries around the world. Recent archaeology
projects took place in Grenada and Wales. Botany projects in
Mexico and marine mammology projects in Canada are other
examples. Volunteers are expected to contribute to the cost
of the research project. Contact the Foundation for Field Research, PO Box 910078, San Diego, CA 92191-0078.

Helpful Publication

Directory of International Internships
Career Development and Placement Services
Michigan State University
113 Student Services Bldg.
East Lansing, MI 48824

STUDY ABROAD

Studying abroad can add a new dimension to your education. Not only can you improve your foreign language skills, you experience a new culture and enjoy the international flavor of learning. Being abroad is also a great way to become truly independent. After my best friend left me in Belgium, I was miserable and felt terribly alone. However, after two days of feeling sorry for myself, I began to enjoy my independence and travel solo. By the time I left the country and came home to America, I had a new perspective on my ability to cope independently. Believe me, it gave me a tremendous sense of power.

Evelyn Trujillo, associate professor of foreign languages at Florida A & M University, feels that studying abroad is an excellent opportunity for students. Students who study abroad become more aware of global affairs and begin to register individual differences between themselves and the residents of foreign countries. In Prof. Trujillo's opinion, students absorb the culture and can thus form their own realistic ideas and opinions of the countries in which they live and study.

There are many things you should consider when deciding to study abroad. For example, you will need to research the various programs and countries in which they are offered. Look at the subject areas and the course credit and determine whether your own university or college will accept the credit. Other considerations are the duration of the program, the costs, housing arrangements, and the financial aid available. Many study abroad programs can be undertaken for the same amount of tuition you pay—or less—at the school you currently attend. Some scholarships are available, and in many cases you can use your financial aid to pay for courses at a university abroad.

Helpful Publications

*Academic Year Abroad
    1996–97*
Sara J. Steen, editor
Institute of International
    Education (IIE)
US Student Programs Division
809 United Nations Plaza
New York, NY 10017-3580

*Development Opportunities
    Catalog*
Overseas Development
    Network
333 Valencia Street
Suite 330
San Francisco, CA 94130

*Directory of Overseas Summer
    Jobs*
Peterson's Guides, Inc.
PO Box 2123
Princeton, NJ 08543-2123
    (609) 243-9111

Summer Jobs in Britain
Peterson's Guides, Inc.
PO Box 2123
Princeton, NJ 08543-2123
    (609) 243-9111

Summer Study Abroad
Peterson's Guides
PO Box 2123
Princeton, NJ 08543-2123

*Vacation Study Abroad: The
    Complete Guide to Summer
    and Short Term Study*
Sara J. Steen, editor
Institute of International
    Education
809 United Nations Plaza
New York, NY 10017-3580

Work in Britain
Council on International
    Educational Exchange
205 East 42nd Street
New York, NY 10017

A Sampling of Study Abroad Programs

American Institute for Study
  Abroad (AIFS)
Programs in Europe, Japan,
  Mexico, Russia
102 Greenwich Avenue
Greenwich, CT 06830
  (800) 727-2437

Beaver College
Center for Education Abroad
Glenside, PA 19038-3295

College Consortium for
  International Studies
2000 P Street, NW, Suite 503
Washington, DC 20036
  (202) 223-0330,
  (800) 453-6956

Council on International
  Educational Exchange
205 East 42nd Street
New York, NY 10017-5706
  (212) 661-1414 ext. 1227

CSA Center for Study Abroad
Study Abroad/Learning
  Vacations
Philip Virtue, Director
2802 E. Madison #160
Seattle, WA 98112
  (206) 726-1498

Division of International
  Programs Abroad
119 Euclid Avenue
Syracuse, NY 13244-0001
  (800) 235-3472

Home and Host International
Carol Grant
2445 Park Avenue S.
Minneapolis, MN 55404
  (800) 768-4388,
  (612) 871-0596

Institute of International
  Education (IIE)
US Student Programs Division
809 United Nations Plaza
New York, NY 10017-3580

Institute for Sport
  Development
Mark M. Huck, Director
US Admissions
1825 I Street, NW, Suite 400
Washington, DC 20006
  (202) 429-6831

IntelCross
International Business: Europe
  in Transition
David E. Calkins
822 College Avenue Box 791
Kentfield, CA 94914-0791
  (800) 788-3922,
  (415) 331-3151

International Student Exchange
  Program (ISEP)
Programs in Asia, Africa,
  Canada, Western and
  Eastern Europe, Latin
  America, and Oceania
3222 N Street, NW, Suite 400
Washington, DC 20007-2489
  (202) 965-0550

International Studies Abroad
817 West 24th Street
Austin, TX 78705
   (512) 480-8522,
   (800) 580-8826

North American Institute for
   Study Abroad
Dr. Michael Currid,
   International Program
   Director
PO Box 279
Riverside, PA 17868
   (717) 275-5099

School for Field Studies
16 Broadway
Beverly, MA 01915-4499
   (508) 927-7777

School for International
   Training
Admissions Office
College Semesters Abroad
Kipling Road, PO Box
   DA1AY
Brattleboro, VT 05302-0676
   (802) 258-3279,
   (800) 336-1616

WorldTeach—Harvard
   Institute for International
   Development
Programs in China, Costa Rica,
   Ecuador, Namibia, Poland,
   Russia, Thailand and South
   Africa
1 Eliot Street
Cambridge, MA 02138
   (617) 495-5527

IMMERSION PROGRAMS
INTENSIVE LANGUAGE STUDY

Immersion programs are designed to help students become fluent in a foreign language. In an immersion program, you live in a foreign country while studying its language, culture, and customs. As you live in the country and become immersed in day to day activities, your verbal responses in the language become quicker and more correct. During your stay, you also are exposed to real-life situations requiring you to use your knowledge of the host country's language and culture.

For many students, particularly those majoring in foreign language, a program such as this is very beneficial because it requires constant practice and use of a language. If you have ever studied a foreign language, you know how difficult it is to become fluent without practice beyond the classroom. For more information on immersion programs, contact your foreign languages department or organizations focusing on international study such as CIEE, the Institute for International Education, or the School for International Training (their addresses are listed on pages 92 and 93).

Intensive language study is similar to an immersion program. With an intensive language study program, you are immersed in the language, culture, and customs of a country, but you may not physically be in the country. If you have a short amount of time and want to be exposed to several levels of a language (from beginning to advanced) quickly, an intensive language study program may be a great option for you.

Immersion Programs

Cuernavaca Language School
Dr. Roberto Alm, Director
PO Box 1011
Kent, Washington 98035-1011   (206) 813-1474

Foreign Language Study Abroad Service
5935 SW 64th Avenue
South Miami, FL 33143   (305) 662-1090, (212) 662-1090

Intensive Language Study Programs

The Center for Central American Development Studies (ICADS)
Dept. 826, Box 025216
Miami, Florida 33102-5216

École de français
Faculté de l'éducation permanente
Université de Montréal
C. P. 6128, succursale A
Montréal, P.Q., Canada H3C 3J7

École des langues vivantes
Faculté des lettres
Pavillon Charles-De Koninck (2305)
Université Laval
P.Q., Canada G1K 7P4

Summer Sessions
Summer Language Institutes
University of California
Department LP
Santa Barbara, CA 93106-2010   (805) 893-7053

OVERSEAS GROUP TOURS

If you have always wanted to visit a foreign country just to see what it's like, you might try going on an overseas group tour. A group tour gives you the opportunity to experience a small taste of a country's culture, history, and beauty. There are several organizations and institutions that organize overseas group tours for students. The foreign language or international studies department at your university may also organize group tours.

Group Tours

Continuing Education
321 Goodison Hall
Eastern Michigan University
Ypsilanti, MI 48197
European Cultural History Tour—Summer and Fall Semester
Asian Cultural History Tour

NAFEO
Lovejoy Building
400 12th Street, NE
Washington, DC 20002

7

LIFE AFTER CLASS

In *Top Performance*, Zig Ziglar, a key motivational speaker, mentions a study conducted jointly by the Stanford Research Institute and the Carnegie Foundation. He emphasizes one of the key findings supported by the study. This finding states: "Fifteen percent of the reason you get a job, keep a job, and move ahead in that job is determined by your technical skills and knowledge . . . regardless of your profession. The other eighty-five percent has to do with your people skills and people knowledge." The best way to gain people knowledge is by dealing with others in some extracurricular activity, thus developing your networking, leadership, and interpersonal skills.

Most college students spend approximately 15 to 18 hours a week in class. That leaves several hours to get involved in extracurricular and other activities with time left for other fun. Extracurricular activities can help you to realize leadership potential you never knew you had. As a participant or a leader in a particular activity, you can develop a sense of teamwork and encounter challenges you might never have found in the classroom. Whether your time is devoted to a sorority, a community group, a sport, or any other activity, you have a unique opportunity for personal development that you can use throughout your life. While you're doing it, you are also developing a diverse base of friends, associates, and contacts with similar interests.

If someone asked me to tell them the most important thing

he should know about a college education, I would tell him that if you are college student and you don't get involved, you haven't really learned a thing. The college education is a full experience. It does not begin with classes and professors and end with a degree and a job. College is a total body experience. You grow in the mind, in the body, and in the spirit. If you don't, then you have missed out. This development can take place in many ways. If you get involved with extra-curricular activities it will continue to pay off long after you've left college. Getting involved not only makes you a more well-rounded individual, it can also help you in finding a job or a new hobby, getting into graduate school, or even meeting your mate. Where other résumés may have gaping holes, loads of white space, or colorful graphics, your résumé will have parliamentarian, student government, junior class officer, member of the basketball team or choir, or resident assistant to enhance and complete it, thus showing you as a well-rounded and mature individual who can handle a variety of activities and still perform academically. This is what both employers and admissions officers at graduate and professional schools want to see. Even if graduate school or a job is not your primary goal, extracurricular activities can be a lot of fun and give you a sense of wholeness. You have the opportunity to enjoy ideas, experiences, and achievements with students who share your interests.

Finding an organization to join, a meeting to attend, or an opportunity to take advantage of should be as simple as taking a leisurely stroll around campus. Each year most campuses hold a fair to acquaint students with the various activities available on campus. Your student activities office also has information about groups on campus, as does your student life handbook. You may also be able to find a list of activities in the college catalog; you can definitely find information on campus bulletin boards. I recently walked around three separate college campuses and picked up no less than fifty flyers, postcards, and bulletins. All of them were advertising campus meetings, new student organizations, volunteer activities, church groups, and so on. Your campus newspaper or radio or television station are other sources for information about groups and upcoming meetings and events. Following are just a few of the organizations you may be able to find and get involved in on your campus or in the community.

Organizations and Activities
Scholastic Honor Societies

Alpha Chi
Alpha Lambda Delta
Alpha Sigma Nu
Gamma Beta Phi
Golden Key

Phi Beta Kappa
Phi Eta Sigma
Phi Kappa Phi
University Honors Program

Honorary Recognition Societies Related to Field of Study

Alpha Beta Gamma
Alpha Epsilon Rho
Alpha Kappa Mu
Alpha Lambda Delta
Alpha Omega Alpha
Alpha Zeta
Beta Kappa Chi
Blue Key
Cardinal Key
Cardinal XX
Chimes
Circle K
Delta Mu Delta
Gamma Beta Phi
Intercollegiate Forensics
Kappa Kappa Pi
Kappa Psi
Lambda Kappa Sigma

Lambda Sigma
Lances Honorary
Mu Phi Epsilon
National Business Honor Society
National Honor Society
Omicron Delta Kappa
Phi Alpha
Phi Beta Kappa
Phi Beta Lambda
Phi Delta Epsilon
Phi Eta Sigma
Phi Kappa Phi
Phi Theta Kappa
Phi Upsilon Omicron
Pi Gamma Mu
Pi Kappa Delta
Pho Chi

Sigma Alpha Iota
Sigma Theta Tau
Society of XI Sigma Pi
Spurs
Talons
Tau Alpha Pi
Tau Beta Sigma
Alpha Epsilon Delta
  (pre-medicine)
Alpha Kappa Delta (sociology)
Beta Alpha Psi (accounting)
Beta Beta Beta (biology)
Beta Gamma Sigma
  (commerce)
Delta Phi Alpha (German)
Eta Kappa Nu
  (electrical engineering)
Eta Sigma Phi (classics)
Kappa Delta Pi (education)
Kappa Mu Epsilon
  (mathematics)
Kappa Tau Alpha (journalism)
Omega Chi Epsilon
  (chemical engineering)

Omicron Delta Epsilon
  (economics)
Phi Alpha Theta (history)
Phi Lambda Upsilon
  (chemistry)
Pi Delta Phi (French)
Pi Kappa Lambda (music)
Pi Mu Epsilon (mathematics)
Pi Sigma Alpha
  (political science)
Pi Tau Sigma
  (mechanical engineering)
Psi Chi (psychology)
Sigma Delta Pi (Spanish)
Sigma Gamma Tau
  (aerospace engineering)
Sigma Pi Sigma (physics)
Sigma Tau Delta (English)
Sigma Xi (scientific research)
Tau Beta Pi (engineering)
Upsilon Pi Epsilon
  (computer science)

Sports and Other Activities

Acting
Baseball
Beauty pageants
Bowling
Campus broadcasting
Campus players
Cheerleading
Chess
Concert band
Crew
Cross country

Dance
Equestrian club
Field hockey
Flag corps
Football
Golf
Gymnastics
Handball
Ice hockey
Intramurals
Jazz band

Judicial board
Karate
Lacrosse
Literary magazine
Majorette
Marching band
Newspaper
Orchestra
Panhellenic council
Pom pom squad
Racquetball

Riflery
Rugby
Soccer
Softball
Swimming
Tennis
Theatre arts
Volleyball
Wrestling
Yearbook

STUDENT HIGHLIGHT

Extracurricular activities rule the life of Jany Allen, a student at Georgia Tech. Here's what she has to say about them.

"As far as extracurricular activities go, I spend more time on those than on my schoolwork! I almost dropped out of Georgia Tech my freshman year to go to Clemson University in Clemson, South Carolina. But I got involved in campus activities at Tech and I'm still here after three years. My freshman year I headed up a program to increase freshman retention rates by pairing up incoming out-of-state students with current students. Because Tech is so technical, and the students are so focused, it can be unfriendly at times. I don't have a technical bone in my body, so I was forced to find nonscience and nonmath programs for 'people, people' like myself. Luckily, Tech is great when it comes to the diversity of its student programs. We have over 250 clubs and organizations. I am most involved in the GT alumni association's student programs. I am president of the student alumni association, a group of approximately 200 students that interact with alumni through programs like the mentor program, externship programs, and the ambassadors, a group of student hosts that give campus tours and keep alumni informed about campus happenings. I am also on the Student Foundation's board of trustees. We manage a $350,000 endowment which funds student groups on campus. The Student Foundation is a philanthropic group that helps to start new clubs and assist current clubs to provide professional development and academic help to their members. My involvement at the alumni association has taught me more than my job or my classes because of the interpersonal relationships that I have built. I also know the value of networking, running an effective meeting, motivating volunteers, as well as business and personal etiquette."

PROFESSIONAL CLUBS/ASSOCIATIONS

Clubs offer numerous opportunities for you as a college student. Within many departments, students majoring in a particular area often form clubs. These clubs serve several functions. For example, within your university's economics department, there may be an economics club whose members hold regular meetings to discuss issues in the department, form study groups for difficult classes, and discuss job opportunities in their field or in the professions in which they are interested. In addition, the club and its members could have their own study or computer room, as is often the case when a majority of the students in a particular department belong to a club. The club may also arrange for workshops, seminars, and visitations with professionals to aid the members. In some instances, the club will attend conferences or participate in competitions as a group effort.

Many students who belong to departmental clubs associated

with a particular profession, such as accounting, economics, engineering, or journalism, will join a corresponding national association such as the National Association of Black Accountants, the American Marketing Association, the National Society of Professional Engineers, or the Society of Professional Journalists. Membership in national organizations can offer numerous extended opportunities. For example, as a member of a national professional organization, you have access to a diverse network of individuals who can assist you in getting your first job after college, in getting into a prestigious graduate school, in setting up your first business, by contributing venture capital for an entrepreneurial effort, by giving advice, or by finding you a mentor. There are associations all over the country, many of them with millions of members. Some of the large national associations maintain job banks for their members. Others hold annual conferences. Many provide newsletters for their members outlining trends in the associated industry, its outlook, and occasionally listing job opportunities and contacts for members to use in a job search. Membership in such an association can also be beneficial if you enter competitions or seek internships, or for those opportunities needing a letter of recommendation, in which case an established association member may be the perfect person to give you one. This would be especially beneficial if you needed the recommendation for something associated with the industry. The member may have special insight to provide you with a recommendation based on the qualities you possess that would be perfect for the opportunity. Another membership benefit is the chance to get a scholarship or fellowship that the association offers to members. If you are not a member of a professional club, association, or similar organization, you should seriously consider joining one. It could help in your future plans, offering that advantage we all could use.

If there isn't a branch of a professional association in which you are interested on campus, consider starting one. Contact the national headquarters of the club or association for more details.

Helpful Publications

Encyclopedia of Associations
Carolyn A. Fischer and Carol A. Schwartz, editors
Gale Research, Inc.
835 Penobscot Building
Detroit, MI 48226-4094   (800) 877-GALE

National Trade and Professional Organizations
of the United States
Columbia Books, Inc.
1212 New York Avenue, NW, Suite 330
Washington, DC 20005   (202) 898-0662

A Sample of Professional Clubs/Associations Frequently Found on College Campuses

American Bar Association
750 N. Lake Shore Drive
Chicago, IL 60611
   (312) 988-5000,
   (800) 621-6159

American Marketing
   Association
250 South Wacker Drive
Chicago, IL 60606
   (312) 648-0536

Association of Collegiate
   Entrepreneurs
Wichita State University
Center for Entrepreneurship
1845 Fairmont
Wichita, KS 67260-0147
   (316) 689-3000

National Society of Black
   Engineers
1454 Duke Street
PO Box 25588
Alexandria, VA 22313-5588
   (703) 549-2207

National Society of Professional
   Engineers
1420 King Street
Alexandria, VA 22314
   (703) 684-2800

Society of Professional
   Journalists
16 S. Jackson
Greencastle, IN 46135
   (317) 653-3333

YOUR CAMPUS MINISTRY

The university campus ministry is an organization devoted to the holistic development of you as an individual. It seeks to enrich your spiritual, physical, intellectual, and social well-being through various programs and activities. Within the campus ministry association, there may be several separate organizations committed to different beliefs such as the Jewish students' association, the Baháí campus ministry, the Baptist campus ministry, the Catholic campus ministry, the Latter Day Saints student association, the Muslim campus ministry, the Orthodox Christian Fellowship, or United College Ministries. The motto of the Florida A & M University campus ministry is "Where heart meets mind." College is an exercise in the stimulation of the mind. If you believe in the need for spiritual guidance as well as educational guidance for total contentment in college, joining the campus ministry association is an excellent way to get both.

In addition to special fellowship and worship, your campus ministry association may offer all or some of the following opportunities:

Bible study
Forums
Support groups
Retreats
Service projects
Social action committees
Study tours
Recreation
Liturgical drama and/or dance
Choir
Prayer room
Spiritual resource room
Daily devotional guide

Orientation magazine
Scholarships and/or loans
Emergency funds
Fellowship dinners
Social events
Dialogues
Voter registration
Leadership development
Newsletter
Discussion groups
Lock-ins
Pastoral counseling
Peace and justice education

OTHER SPIRITUAL ORGANIZATIONS

There are also independent fellowship groups which may or may not be on your campus. If you are interested in joining, obtaining information, or starting one of these groups on your campus, write to the addresses below for more information.

Campus Crusade for Christ International (CCC)
100 Sunport Lane
Orlando, FL 32809   (407) 826-2131

Fellowship of Christian Athletes
8701 Leeds Road
Kansas City, MO 64129   (816) 921-0909

Inter-Varsity Christian Fellowship of the United States of
    America (IVCF)
PO Box 7895
Madison, WI 53707-7895   (608) 274-9001

8

FUN WITHIN THE WALLS

An important factor in your happiness in college is the amount of entertainment and fun that you seek. Some of you may be saying, to your parents' approving nods, "If I party too hard, I might flunk out." That is true, but if you don't have any fun at all, you may bore yourself into depression. As they say, "All work and no play. . . ." The trick to having an excellent academic record along with loads of fun is to achieve a balance between education and entertainment. Although it may be a tenuous balance, it is possible. My personal philosophy while at college was to work hard and play hard. To do this, I dedicated the majority of my weekdays to getting an education in the classroom and my weekends to getting a life. If you're wondering what fun and entertainment have to do with getting the most out of a college education, let me clarify one major point: entertainment and fun are not synonymous with partying and alcohol. Entertainment is any activity that allows the body and mind to relax and you to enjoy being alive and well in the world. It could include a walk in the park, attending a music recital, theater performance, or football game, listening to a speech by a political activist or famous actor, or just having an informal get-together among friends. The benefits of entertainment are many. First and most important, it is your chance to relax. Second, wherever there are people, you automatically have a valuable playing field to develop possible contacts. You can find out about job opportunities, or even meet a future partner for a business venture at an informal gathering or other social outing. You can trade ideas, thoughts, opinions, and dreams. Finally, you could meet the person with whom you would like to share your life.

SPECIAL INTEREST CLUBS

Special interest clubs are formed based on the common interests or backgrounds of the members. Some of the clubs are associated with a specific city or metropolitan area. For instance, some schools have a DC Metro Club, an Ohio Club, an Atlanta Club, and so on. Such clubs usually organize parties, car washes, study sessions, trips home, and newsletters. At the very least these clubs can provide excellent networking opportunities for you. Other members can put you in touch with the best professors and in general help orient you to life on the college campus.

Other special interest clubs are formed on the basis of cultural heritage or country of origin like the Haitian, Jewish, and African Studies or the Caribbean Association. In these organizations the individual has many opportunities to delve deeper into his or her heritage or background. The clubs also offer networking opportunities, as well as theme parties, group study sessions, organized trips to associated countries, and lots of fun with people who share a common background.

BECOMING A GREEK

Greek societies are national corporations with local chapters set up under the direction of the college or university where they are located. Joining a Greek organization can give you a very active social life filled with parties, community activities, and many other programs sponsored by the organization. At many colleges and universities, there are sorority and fraternity houses in which you can live. In these houses you will find a challenging and usually exciting atmosphere and—at times— household chores. This type of communal living often results in significantly lower housing costs as compared to dorm or apartment living.

There are several advantages to joining a fraternity or sorority. When you join you often have immediate and continuous opportunities for social interaction. Most sororities and fraternities have a continuous calendar of events and parties scheduled for the entire year and are constantly thinking up new ones. Many of the community events the sorority or fraternity participates in will make a helpful addition to your résumé. A sorority or fraternity is also an excellent way to develop an extensive network of contacts made up of members past and present, which can help you in many endeavors ranging from finding a job to getting a recommendation for graduate school to getting advice or funds for a big project you are undertaking. As a member, you may also have access to old class handouts on courses, tests, study notes, syllabi, and reference material. Scholarships are sometimes available to you as a member of the fraternity or sorority. And once you become a member, you gain a group of associates with many smaller common interests and a big one—the fraternity or sorority.

COLLEGE PASTIMES

You will find many entertaining pastimes while at college. For example, there are often fraternity and sorority parties that you can attend. At Florida A & M, there were before-Thanksgiving parties, before-Christmas parties, before-the-finals parties, after-the-finals parties, Spring Break jams, and many other excuses to relax. If you aren't a member of a fraternity or sorority you are still welcome to attend—many such parties are open to the general public, although both fraternities and sororities may charge a small fee. At Florida A & M, 25-cent and 50-cent parties were popular. Most Greek organizations use the parties to raise funds for charitable activities.

For the sports fiend, there are many events you can watch while at college. These events are usually free to students. I loved going to football games. Only *I* never watched the games, I was too busy watching our band, the Marching 100. You will find a variety of sporting events at any college—basketball games, swimming events, baseball games, wrestling matches, and many other athletic competitions, depending on what your school offers.

If you like to eat and watch movies, and live in a dormitory, pizza parties and dorm movie nights will be a fun activity for you. Several residents can share the expense of renting movies and buying pizzas or, as was the case in my dormitory on several occasions, the pizza and the movies were generously provided by the resident assistant or university.

Recreation in the form of exercise is very easy to accomplish at college. Most campuses encompass acres of land, so walking is one way to exercise and relax. Most campuses also have gyms and fitness centers, so you can work out there. You may also be able to join an aerobics or other type of fitness class. You might want to learn karate or tae kwon do, if your university offers them.

The student union is another entertainment option. You can play video games in the game room, talk with friends in the lounge, or, if your union has one, go to the campus club or eatery for an appetizer and a drink to unwind.

If you're interested in more cultural entertainment, you could attend a play performed by the theater group, watch a dance recital, or listen to a poetry reading. Musical performances by your institution's jazz ensemble group or gospel choir are another option.

Concerts, step shows, and other major events will often be

sponsored by the student activities office or the student government association. Boyz II Men, Bill Cosby, and many other
performers visited our campus.

Opportunities for entertainment are abundant on most college campuses. There's always something to do and someone to
do it with. It really depends on your idea of entertainment.

9

WORKING AROUND CAMPUS

There are many jobs on a college campus. Some can be long-term, like working as a librarian's assistant throughout an entire college career, or they can be short-term, like being a testing assistant for a required campuswide test for one day. Campus jobs can be just as exciting and beneficial as an internship. With them, you can acquire networking and interpersonal skills and develop contacts. In addition, having relevant work experience is often the difference between successful and unsuccessful job applicants and can likewise be a key factor in your admission to a graduate or professional school.

A job on your college campus not only provides experience for you, it can expose you to some very important opportunities and people. A job on campus literally could change the direction of your life. Picture this: You work in your dean's office as a staff assistant. The CEO and president of a major corporation has accepted an invitation to speak at your school. When he arrives in the office, you greet him and chat with him for a couple of minutes before he joins the dean for breakfast. Just before leaving the office, he offers you an internship with his company for the summer because he was so impressed with your insightful conversation. Think this is impossible? Think again. Not only is it possible, it happened several times to students during my undergraduate years at Florida A & M University. At the school of business and industry, presidents and

CEOs of Fortune 500 companies visited the school on a weekly basis. They and the recruiters who often accompanied them gave speeches and held receptions, and frequently offered internships and co-op opportunities to interested and interesting students.

Gaining valuable work experience is one advantage of getting a job in college, but there are many others: getting references for your future career, adding attractive features to your résumé, acquiring a mentor, and acquiring technical and leadership skills. Depending on the organization, for some jobs you may be able to get credit toward your college degree. In fact, some jobs are created specifically for that reason. That is called cooperative education, and it was discussed in chapter 5.

Work study is another kind of job. The work study program is jointly sponsored by the federal government and your college to offer part-time employment—the government subsidizes the wages paid by the college. Work study is available on most college campuses primarily for students as part of their financial aid packages. Work study jobs can be anywhere on a college campus including the bookstore, a lab, or the public relations office. With planning, you can obtain work study in an office where you will be able to gain valuable contacts and experience that could help you when participating in contests, applying for a job, or applying to graduate school. For example, a student who aspires to be photojournalist can work on the campus newspaper. While there, she will get experience, résumé credits, and a portfolio of pictures and articles, and be able to participate in journalism contests. In addition, the advisor for the newspaper can help by critiquing her work and sharing real world experiences with her.

COMMUNITY SERVICE/VOLUNTEER

Community service is important for college students not only for the experience and the opportunity to help the community, but also because it may result in financial aid or college credit.

Community service can also add new depth to a résumé or a personal statement for graduate school. In addition, many friends and associates as well as valuable business or social contacts can be made at events benefiting individuals within a community.

Campus Compact, a coalition of more than 500 colleges and universities, is an organization that aids students in their community efforts. Over 539,000 students participate in this program. Some colleges and universities offer financial aid in exchange for community service with this program. For more information, write to Campus Compact, c/o Brown University, Box 1975, Providence, RI 02912, (401) 863-1119.

The Campus Outreach Opportunity League (COOL) is another national community service organization that promotes student participation. The organization works with students and faculty at over 650 colleges and universities and sponsors regional workshops and national conferences. For further information, write to COOL, 1101 15th Street, NW, Suite 203, Washington, DC 20005, (202) 296-7010.

Other Volunteer Organizations

Habitat for Humanity
121 Habitat Street
Americus, GA 31709   (912) 924-6935

Project America
PO Box 1901
Richmond, VA 23215   (800) 880-3352

Points of Light Foundation
1737 H Street, NW
Washington, DC 20006   (202) 273-9186, (800) 879-5400

Volunteers of America
3939 N. Causeway Blvd.
Metairie, LA 70002   (504) 837-2652, (800) 899-0089

STUDENT HIGHLIGHT

AJ Robinson is a student who is seriously involved in his community. He's been doing good works since he began his college career at Stanford University. He is now a graduate student at Harvard University studying political science. "I was the co-founder and co-director of a student-run, nonprofit organization designed to empower economically disadvantaged youth from the San Francisco Bay Area. The program was entitled SOAR (Students Offering Alternative Realities) and the kids we worked with ranged in age from 14 to 18. We provided academic tutoring, job training, professional counseling, peer mentoring, and summer jobs. We also conducted an SAT prep class and a host of other weekend workshops. The organization had a staff of approximately 25 to 40, depending on the mood and commitment level of the students at Stanford. Community service has changed my life by teaching me the politics behind poverty. It also taught me how to motivate and mobilize a large and diverse population."

PROFESSIONAL TRADE EXPERIENCE

Your trade is your eventual occupation. Professional trade experience can be gained by joining any of the numerous campus organizations that practice your trade or profession as part of the activities associated with your campus. For example, most college campuses have a yearbook, newspaper, radio station, television station, student government, and literary magazine. As a staff member for one of these organizations you can enjoy many benefits, not the least of which is getting work experience to use when you actually enter the job market. Becoming a part of these organizations could get easily get you a job, internship, or co-op in the appropriate industry. You can also gain valuable contacts through your advisor, who may have already worked as a professional in the television, radio, magazine, or newspaper industry. Likewise, if you are interested in diplomacy and politics, student government offers opportunities. The advisor for student government may also have once been professionally ensconced in politics on a local, state, or federal government level. The individuals you meet while a part of these campus organizations may be able to offer numerous contacts, referrals, and information for furthering your own career. They can serve as excellent sources for advice, mentoring, and recommendations.

You can also participate in contests, attend conferences, forums, and other meetings or retreats associated with your trade. Retreats are usually held for the members of an organization in a popular and occasionally exotic location. During a retreat, meetings and discussions are held on topics of concern to the group members and the university. Organizations may also host a career fair specifically for interested students in their groups.

To get the most out of a job in one of these areas, you could try tying your work study in to one of these organizations. Doing this means that you could be paid to do something you really enjoy and that you think of as your future career!

Some of the staff positions in these campus organizations offer low salaries. While often enjoying relaxing fringe benefits like retreats, student government officials such as president and vice president often get paid a stipend of as much as $10,000 a year and sometimes more.

STUDENT HIGHLIGHTS

Rondre Jackson is a senior political education and history major at the University of California at Los Angeles. He relates his personal experience to his campus job.

"I am a well-rounded student who doesn't just study. I socialize, get involved in many activities, and work, all of which really enhance my college experience. There are activities in particular that make college rather fun for me. The main ones are: working for the basketball gym (Pauley Pavilion) and being the manager of UCLA's women's basketball team. I firmly believe that students should have some work experience while going to school because college is usually the last step before entering the real world of work. A job in college can help you gain experience to prepare for entering this reality.

"I chose to work at Pauley Pavilion because of a deep interest in sports, especially basketball. As an employee, my job mainly offers behind-the-scenes work. However it has huge advantages. I watch and go to all of UCLA's games and sports-related events for free. To me this is the best part, particularly when the men's basketball team went to and won the Final Four in 1995. The excitement and adrenaline at that event and just about all the games is exhilarating.

"Earlier during my college career, while I was working for Pauley Pavilion, I was able to get acquainted with the coaches for the women's basketball team. Later I interviewed for the position of manager with the women's basketball team and got it. Being employed as the first male manager of UCLA's women's basketball team began to make my college experience even more unique and quite interesting. As the manager of the team, I began to travel extensively to places like Alaska, Texas,

Oregon, Massachusetts, and many other states to which I had never been.

"Even though traveling with the team and visiting all these places and more is a big plus for my job, the friendships made with the players and coaches of the team are even more special than the excitement of traveling. As a manager almost completely surrounded by women, I began to gain a new perspective on the way females should be treated. I now feel like I have an extended family of sisters I'll remember forever.

"Not only have I become a well-seasoned traveler, and a male sensitive to the needs of women, I have also picked up a lot of organizational skills that I feel will really help me in the real world. Managing a team includes many organizational and scheduling activities such as handling and ordering uniforms, arranging study hall, and preparing for meals. My job on campus opened up a whole new world for me and I love it!"

Rondre offers his personal tips for getting the most out of a college education:

- "Don't wait until the last minute. A lot of surviving in college is based on organizational-related activities. Time management for every type of situation is a must. If I hadn't been a good manager of my time, there is no way I could have done so much as the manager of the women's basketball team."
- "Do take advantage of the services and activities provided while in college such as career placement and counseling. College tuition can be very expensive yet all kinds of services are provided. If you use them, that will definitely help you feel that you have gotten the most out of your college experience and the most for your buck."

"After graduating, think about the things that you got the most out of in college and use those skills as decision makers to make choices for life after college. For example, I have really enjoyed being a manager for the basketball team. Although I still have a strong interest in attending law school after I graduate, I am considering becoming a coach for a few years, either at UCLA or another college or university. I certainly have the contacts and have developed the skills for it. In any case I will have my degree, have many friends and contacts, have many special memories, and have the experience of managing a team for a major university."

10

THE STUDENT ENTREPRENEUR

There are budding entrepreneurs on college campuses all over the world. You may even have an entrepreneurial bone hidden in your body. If you think about it, a college campus is one of the best places to start a fledgling business. A campus is a tightly knit, concentrated world within which, with the right product or service, you have a receptive potential clientele. All you need is a good idea, the willingness to do a little work, and a friendly personality. An entrepreneurial business venture in college could produce money to help pay for your tuition bill, your living expenses, a new car, investments for your future, a Christmas present for your significant other, or your dream trip to Hawaii. Your business would also show potential employers and graduate school admissions officers not only what an enterprising individual you are, but that you have initiative, maturity, responsibility, and innovativeness.

For a great idea geared to college students (individuals between the age of 17 and 25), campus is a perfect, ready-made marketplace. Many students are eager to try new things, and because most of them are away from home and must find someone to provide various services cheaply, college is an excellent atmosphere for a low-cost, low-overhead service business. Don't neglect a potential side market, composed of campus faculty and staff members and older college students. Although the older market may be less a target for you, it's never a good idea to automatically assume no interest.

In addition to an instant market, you have access to campus bulletin boards, dormitories, perhaps radio and TV stations, friends who can and need to work, and professors willing and able to give advice. You may also have the option of taking classes in entrepreneurship, marketing, advertising, financial and managerial accounting, the legal environment of business, commercial law, and so forth if you need additional information and development to run your new business. Some schools, such as George Mason University in Fairfax, Virginia, maintain an entrepreneurship office on campus to aid budding small business owners.

Advertising

Most colleges and universities have bulletin boards all over campus, the perfect place for budding entrepreneurs to tout their services or products. Or you may want to hang creative flyers on doorknobs to dorm rooms and faculty offices. On some campuses you may need to consult the student government office to make sure that you can post flyers about your business. However, even if that is not permitted, a creative and agile mind can find alternatives for advertising the business. For example, never underestimate the power of word of mouth advertising, which can be provided by your partners in the business, the people you hire to work for you, or, most effective of all, satisfied customers to whom you've given free services or samples of your product as a way of introducing your business.

On many campuses there are also radio stations, television stations, and newspapers. For a small fee or perhaps for free, you could advertise your business in one of those media. Don't be afraid to ask both the students who work there and their advisors, who are usually professors or individuals who have worked in the communications industry, for assistance in preparing your newspaper ad, broadcast message, or commercial.

Advice

Starting a business raises a lot of questions and issues. Since many of the professors on campus may already own or have started a business in the past, a lot of those questions can most likely be answered quickly and easily by visiting the office of such a professor. If he or she can't help, he or she will probably know someone who can. And if your business lasts throughout the year, many of the accounting and economics professors will gladly assist you in preparing your taxes. If your business is successful enough to make a profit and reach one of your goals, such as paying tuition or the car note, and still leave you with enough for other purposes, certain professors are also good resources for advice on investment vehicles for your money. You may want to consider a class on investments or financial management.

Where Do I Get the Money to Pay Start-up Costs?

If you have a product to sell, you may need money for the materials to produce it. There are several rules you should follow if you have a product-based business.

- Devise several ways to make the product. Research it thoroughly to find the most inexpensive way to create a quality product.
- Remember, time is also money! If it takes you a long time to make the product, you may want to reconsider your idea or approach.
- If you think your idea is really revolutionary, you may need to patent or copyright it; at that point you should seek professional advice.
- Start small. Don't make more than one or two samples of the product.
- To advertise, show the item to friends and to staff and faculty members with whom you have a good relationship. If

they like it, word of mouth will help sell your product in the beginning.

- Get advance payment for orders. If you sell enough, you may be able to pay for production of a large amount. If your product requires outside suppliers, you may be able to get a discount for large orders—be sure to ask.
- Do not pay someone to help you unless you can afford it—until you show a profit, you probably can't. Your friends may help you for free as a favor or they could become your partners and share in both the expenses and the profits.
- Do not let your business, no matter how successful, overshadow the real reasons you're at college: to learn and have fun. Even though your business is a form of learning for you, you must remember that you are in college and one of your major goals should be to graduate, which it will be extremely hard to do if you don't go to class and forget to study. You must also remember to have fun. Don't fall into the trap of all work and no play. Not only is this dull and unsociable, it's unhealthy.

If you have a service business, your start-up costs should be less than if you were manufacturing a product. You are the product. Since you are already made and finished, as it were, you do not need to pay for materials. However, you may need to pay for equipment to service your customers. For example, if you decide to offer manicures, you might need files, fingernail polish remover, polish, and so on. To advertise a service business, you may need to do a lot of work for free, since you do not have a physical product to show. Also, depending on the nature of your business, you may need business cards and flyers, which you can have printed for a minimal fee at most print shops. After you've got these, you can go to work!

The following are some typical businesses that students start on campus.

The Mini Beauty Salon

A mini beauty salon is fairly easy and low cost to set up. Consider the following example:

Printing flyers for dormitory bulletin boards $10

Equipment—nail files, buffing pads, polish, nails, etc. $30

Note: Before opening a salon, consult with the dorm counselor for regulations regarding this type of business—it may not be allowed on your campus.

Real Estate—Converting Homes into Student Apartments

This idea requires more capital. However, if your parents can help you obtain a mortgage and provide credit references, then this is an excellent and viable idea. You can obtain a small, two- or three-bedroom home with approximately $2,000 as a down payment and a monthly mortgage payment of roughly $575. (Of course, these figures depend on the city in which the house is located.) You could live in one of the rooms and rent out the others for approximately $400 per room. This would allow you the freedom to pay utilities, taxes, and the mortgage for the house, and still provide a little extra income for you and your parents. After you graduate, you could keep the house as an investment and continue to rent it to students, or you could sell it.

This is a venture that must be carefully planned. First, look for a structurally sound house that will not require a lot of money to fix it up. If you plan to rent your house, you must make sure that it meets the requirements of the local code officials for electricity, plumbing, heating, and gas. It is a good idea to wait until you have attended your university for a year or more. This way you will know the town and its most desirable locations and will have some idea of the market value of the house in which you are interested and the amount students would be willing to pay for a room in it. If you're handy with tools and fixing things, be on the lookout for government auctions listed in the newspaper and on signs around town. Although many of these houses are fixer-uppers and some may be located in less desirable sections of the city, at some auctions you can buy a house for as little as $2,000. Other ways to acquire an inexpensive house include VA repossessions, foreclosures, and houses that have been on a realtor's list for over a year. Just bear in mind the costs you'll need to spend to make the house livable.

Résumé Preparation

To prepare résumés, you need a computer or a fairly sophisticated word processor, or you may be able to camp out in one of your campus computer labs (bearing in mind that other students need to do their schoolwork there). You should be fairly proficient with software programs such as Microsoft Word or WordPerfect. Ask the career center staff to recommend business to you.

Typing and Professional Services

Type a research paper, create a business card, or proofread a short story. You can do any of these with a word processor and a proficiency in English.

Storage Services

Several students on my campus, those who had apartments locally or were from the area, got together to provide storage services for students who lived far away and could not take their belongings home over the summer. This is an ideal and effortless moneymaker for students who have signed a long-term lease but may be leaving for the summer, or whose roommate is leaving.

Other Student Business Ideas

Dating services	Graphic designers
Apartment locators and sublease finders	Beauty consultants (Mary Kay, Avon)

Helpful Publications

How To Set Up Your Own Small Business
by Max Fallek
The American Institute of Small Business
7515 Wayzata Boulevard, Suite 201
Minneapolis, MN 55426   (612) 545-7001

The Ted Nicholas Small Business Course: A Step By Step Guide to Starting and Running Your Own Business
by Ted Nicholas
Dearborn Financial Publishing, Inc.
520 North Dearborn Street
Chicago, IL 60610-4354

STUDENT HIGHLIGHT

Running down the field to catch the perfect pass or across center court to shoot the winning three-pointer is a way of life for Scott Price, an economics major at Florida A & M University (FAMU). As president and owner of Flagstik Productions, a small photography business, Scott is always a part of the action and poised to shoot—with his camera, of course. For over three years, Scott has used his love of sports and photographer's eye to grow his business into a profitable enterprise. Even though Scott spends most of his time snapping pictures, he always finds time for golf, his favorite sport. His photo business card, which he says is essential for the professional photographer, features a picture of him playing golf and the slogan "Possessing a photographer's eye with a golfer's touch."

Although he has been taking pictures since the age of six, Scott didn't decide to use photography as a money-making vehicle until college, when he began working for two of FAMU's campus publications. While taking pictures for the Rattler Yearbook and the FAMUAN newspaper, Scott's pictures were noticed by an aspiring model who asked him to photograph her. When he presented the pictures to her, she was so pleased, she told others, who then approached Scott. Seeing the power of his position as photographer for two major campus publications, Scott began to promote his business through them. For Scott, making contacts and positive word-of-mouth advertising were the key factors in his success. In his words, "It's not what you know, but who you know." In his sophomore year, he approached the FAMU Athletic Department and since then, shooting memorable sports moments and senior athlete portraits has become the major focus of his business, although Scott continues to take pictures of aspiring models. One of his modeling pictures is scheduled to appear in *Jet* magazine for the beauty of the week photo. Still, Scott never rests. He also participates in photo contests. He won best photo of the month twice and $150.00 in *U, The College Magazine*'s photography contest.

Scott's business in a college town is profitable for many reasons. Scott explains: "Having two major universities in one city creates a gigantic market of customers for me." Whenever he wants to advertise, he posts flyers in all the dormitories and high student traffic areas, then distributes them by hand to people walking on campus. He also uses other campus resources to his advantage. For instance, he has appeared on *Snake Eyes*, FAMU's weekly television show. And in exchange for free photos of special athletic events, *The Capital Outlook*, a small local newspaper, runs his advertisements.

Why does Scott do it? "Although my business helps to pay a lot of my school expenses, my main goal for my income and the exposure from my photography is to fund and further my professional golfing career after college," he explains.

11

THE COLLEGE INVESTOR

Wouldn't it be nice to graduate from college virtually debt free, or with at least a little money in the bank and a couple of investments on the side? Many of you who are burdened with student loans may feel that this is impossible. But it is possible. In fact, it's quite probable, if you use the techniques of sound financial management. They may not make you wealthy and you may not be totally debt free, but at least you'll have some investments, perhaps a savings account, a couple of savings bonds, and maybe a mutual fund account or a certificate of deposit (CD). Even as a college student on a very tight budget, you can save a little money, have a decent size bank account, and maybe enough left over to try a few conservative investments.

First you need a little money. Let's think about it. The average fast food order is approximately $4. If you eat at a fast food restaurant an average of three times a week, that comes to 12 times per month, or approximately 144 times per year—that's $576 a year spent just for fast food. If you gave in to only one fast food craving per week, you could save $384 in a year. If you take advantage of coupons you could save even more. In Tallahassee, where I went to college, there were at least three coupon books sent to students every week filled with coupons for Burger King, Subway, McDonald's, haircuts, and many other items.

You could use the $8 per week ($32 per month) you save by

avoiding McDonald's, Burger King, and Taco Bell to accumulate $384 in savings by the end of the year. If you added another $25 dollars to your monthly savings, $6.25 per week, your savings would increase by $300, to give you a grand total of $684 at the end of one year. At the end of four years, without even investing your money, you would have saved $2,736! Of course, you'd have to keep the money somewhere, so you might put it in a savings account at your bank. Interest is minimal and usually can be earned only if you maintain a certain balance, which varies by bank. Or you could wisely invest it in savings bonds, mutual funds, CDs, or stocks, discussed later in this and the next chapter.

Let's consider your bank account, which could cost rather than earn you money if you don't shop around for the right one. Most banks charge fees and require minimum balances. Look for a bank that has either low or no fees. Otherwise, you could end up paying maintenance fees just to have the account, write checks, withdraw your money, or use an ATM. There are some banks—particularly in cities with a high percentage of college students—that will establish accounts specifically catering to students' needs. For example, they may not require a minimum balance, or they will allow you to write a limited number of checks per month or have unlimited use of their ATM, for a small monthly fee.

Credit unions are nonprofit cooperative financial institutions that are operated exclusively for the benefit of their members. The union is usually composed of people from the same group such as company employees, members of labor unions or church groups. Therefore, their primary goal is not to make a profit but to serve their members. Most of them allow you to write unlimited checks and maintain a low balance in your checking and savings accounts, and they offer more money-saving options. If you are able to join a credit union, do so. If you or your parents belong to a credit union at home, you might be able to extend your membership to one in the city where your college is located. It will save you over the long run.

You should establish a good relationship with your bank at college. Don't bounce checks and keep a reasonable balance well above the minimum required. Don't make frequent withdrawals. A good relationship with your bank will be helpful when you need loans (either business or car) and low-fee credit cards.

Now that we've found you some money to invest, let's discuss a few investment options.

MUTUAL FUNDS

What Are Mutual Funds?

Mutual funds are vehicles for people who don't have large amounts of money to invest. For as little as $100, you can invest in a mutual fund. Some who opt for an automatic investment plan can invest for as little as $25 in mutual funds such as Twentieth Century Ultra. Although the initial investment is much lower, participating in an automatic investment plan requires that you invest a certain amount every month. This amount is usually deducted electronically from your checking or savings account. To establish a fund, mutual fund companies pool the monies of all the small investors and invest the total in numerous stocks, bonds, T-bills, and elsewhere. Each fund has a manager or group of managers who decide where to invest. Depending on the type of investments the manager chooses, the fund can be classified as aggressive, aggressive growth, balanced, or conservative, classifications based on how risky the fund may be and the fluctuation in its worth. In simple terms, I think of it as how easily I could lose all the money that I have invested. The riskier and more aggressive the fund, the more your shares will probably grow in worth—or the more they may decrease in worth. A conservative fund will grow, but at a slow, steady rate and in smaller increments. An aggressive fund could grow rapidly and with wild fluctuations, plummeting one year and skyrocketing the next. With aggressive funds, there is usually a significant, steady increase over the long term (5 to 10 years), compared with small increases over the short term (3 to 5 years) with conservative mutual funds. As a young investor who has years before retirement, you may want to consider an aggressive fund. If you want to invest only for a few years (you think you may need the money after college, for instance), you'd do better with more conservative funds.

Terms You Should Know

- Load—A sales charge that can range anywhere from 2 to 9 percent. The load could be "front end," meaning you pay the charge when you purchase shares of a fund, or "back end," meaning you pay the charge when you sell shares of a fund. A "no-load" fund is free of these sales charges, but you may face other fees.
- Net asset value (N.A.V.)—The price of the fund per share minus the fund's expenses.
- Prospectus—A brochure or booklet containing information about the investment objectives, risks, fees, and management of a fund. This is a legal document and should be read by investors interested in purchasing shares of a fund before taking any action.
- Return—The percentage yield of your investment or its gain in value.
- Investment objectives—A description of the fund's investment plans and goals.
- Management fees—Fees that a fund pays to its investment adviser or manager.

Which Fund Should You Invest In?

If you have only a limited amount to invest in a mutual fund, then your choice will be reduced from the approximately 5,000 mutual funds that are available to about 300 or fewer. Although you may have to find a fund that will allow you to invest small amounts of money, such funds can still be high-quality investments. Also, some funds that require minimum investments of $1,000 or more may allow you to make an initial investment of $50 or less if you enroll in a monthly automatic investment plan. Once you have determined how much you can afford to invest and where you'd like to invest it, call that company's 800 number and ask for a prospectus. When it arrives, read it thoroughly. Also, many books are available to help you understand fully how mutual funds work. Peruse magazines such as *Fortune*, *Money*, *Kiplinger's Personal Finance*, *Forbes*, *Business Week*, and others to become an informed investor.

Helpful Publication

Getting Started in Mutual Funds
John D. Wiley & Sons
Professional, Reference, and Trade Group
605 Third Avenue
New York, NY 10158-0012

A Few No-Load Mutual Funds with Initial Investments of $250

Berger 100 Fund	(800) 333-1001
Berger 101 Fund	(800) 333-1001
Berger Small Company Growth Fund	(800) 333-1001
AmTrust Value	(800) 532-1146
MIM Stock Appreciation	(800) 233-1240
Strong Total Return	(800) 368-1030
Strong Investment	(800) 368-1030

STUDENT HIGHLIGHT

During 1993, my friend Cadeltra Adams and I decided to invest in the Berger Family of Mutual Funds. Cadeltra invested in the Small Company Growth Fund and I invested in the Berger One Hundred Mutual Fund. Since then, her initial investment has increased by approximately 74 percent. My investment didn't do quite as well, initially increasing by only approximately 10 percent. It has begun to perform much better recently, however. The Berger Small Company Growth Fund is riskier and more aggressive than the Berger One Hundred Fund. As such, on average the potential for an investment in the Small Company Growth will be better.

SAVINGS BONDS

Savings bonds are a popular choice for investors with smaller amounts of money. They are easy to purchase—available at any bank. They are obtainable for minimal amounts. Series EE bonds are available in denominations ranging from $50 to $10,000, for half their face value. That is, you can purchase a $50 savings bond for $25. The bond reaches full maturity (it's worth $50) in 12 years; however, it can be cashed after you have held it for six months. If you hold it for five years, it will have earned a market-based rate of 6 percent. Since the bonds are issued and backed by the U.S. government, they are a safe investment—you are essentially lending the government money, and as such, your investment will *never* be worthless.

If you want a safe, steady investment, savings bonds are for you. Although they will not make you rich quickly, they will help you to save money and deter you from spending it needlessly. If you bought a $50 savings bond (at $25) monthly for four years, you would have saved $1,200, not including the interest the bonds accrue. Although it may not seem like a lot, it could be the down payment for a new car, or it could come in handy when you move to a new city.

Helpful Publication

U.S. Savings Bonds: A Comprehensive Guide
  for Bond Owners and Financial Professionals
Daniel J. Pederson
TSBI Publishing
PO Box 9249
Detroit, MI 48209   (313) 843-1910

CERTIFICATES OF DEPOSIT

If you happen to get a windfall of at least $500, you might consider buying a certificate of deposit (CD). A CD is a receipt issued by a bank for money placed in a special type of savings account for periods ranging from one month to ten years. Money invested in CDs usually gets a higher rate of interest than that in a regular savings account. The more money you invest and the longer you leave it in, the higher the interest rate will be on your money.

12

BUILDING A BLUE-CHIP
STOCK PORTFOLIO

It's been said for years: It takes money to make money. In most cases that's true, especially to make large amounts. However, with a little investment savvy, even college students who typically survive on a shoestring budget that dictates minimal furniture, dates, and endless boxes of macaroni and cheese can invest a little money in stocks. Even for students on scholarships or financial aid, there is money to be found for investment purposes if you really want to do it.

If you're telling yourself right now that the author of this book is totally crazy because you have no money and can barely pay for school, then maybe you need to become an enterprising entrepreneur (see chapter 10) or maybe you should reassess your budget. You'll be surprised to see where some of your money is going without your realizing it. One of my friends and I looked at our spending habits for one month and discovered that 45 percent of our excess cash was going to fast food, the beauty parlor, and other luxuries. Read how to save just by cutting back on fast food in chapter 11.

To build your portfolio of blue-chip stocks you first need to thoroughly research the companies in which you are interested. For example, if you like drinking Coca-Cola or Pepsi, start by researching those companies as potential investments. After creating a list of companies, visit your campus or local library for the history and financial information of those companies.

Assess each company's performance and earnings over a period of time (at least five years). Most important, look for information on each company's dividend reinvestment plan (DRIP) or optional cash purchase plan (OCP). You also need to look at each company's dividend payout and dividend growth potential. At this point, if a company doesn't have a DRIP, doesn't accept OCPs, and pays a minimal dividend with no growth potential, you do not want it on your list. As a college student on a tight budget, you may not be able to consistently purchase stocks of the company on the open market. You would have to do this if they don't accept OCPs. If they don't have a DRIP, then dividends that you earn on the shares of stock you own will not be reinvested. Therefore, although your shares of stock may increase in value, they won't do it through dividends. Dividend earnings will be very important for your portfolio.

Since most college students have little time to devote to continuous research and tracking stocks by the minute, trying to pick a stock that will grow by leaps and bounds in value is risky and time consuming. If you choose the stock of a well-established company with a record of paying dividends, you can invest and relax. Over time, stocks have proven to be the most profitable investment choice. Don't be alarmed by the rising and falling values of your stock. Invest, sit back, and watch it grow. If you want to continue reinvesting in your portfolio, invest the same amount at approximately the same time every month, quarter, or year; this is called dollar cost averaging. A steady investment of the same amount at fixed intervals allows you to purchase more of your company's stock when it has decreased in value and less stock when it has increased in value. Over time, it all averages out and your investment will continue to grow.

TERMS YOU SHOULD KNOW

DRIP—DRIP is an acronym that stands for dividend reinvestment plan. A dividend reinvestment plan is offered by companies to allow their stockholders to automatically reinvest dividend payments in additional shares of the company's stock. Dividend reinvestment is normally an inexpensive way of purchasing additional shares of company stock since the fees are usually lower or may be completely absorbed by the company.

OCP—OCP is an acronym for optional cash purchase or payment. This is when a shareholder purchases additional shares of company stock directly through the company.

Blue-chip stocks—High quality investments with lower risk than most average stocks in the market. Blue chips are usually stocks of companies with a long history of earnings and dividend payments. For example, IBM and Walt Disney are examples of blue-chip stock.

Some companies, such as Exxon Corporation, have started Shareholder Investment Plans (SIPs) or direct purchase programs that allow you to purchase your first share of stock and every share directly from the company. You must make an initial investment in the plan ranging anywhere from $25 to $500 or more.

If you want to diversify your portfolio immediately or the company in which you want to invest doesn't have a SIP or direct purchase program, you will have to use a broker to buy a minimum of one share of the company's stock. Most companies require that an individual be a current holder of at least one share of stock before allowing him or her to participate in a DRIP or make an OCP.

For small dollar amounts, companies such as A. G. Edwards, Smith Barney, and Dean Witter Reynolds will purchase and register one share of stock for you on the stock market. You can usually call one of their local offices. (See the list at the end of this section for others.)

When you buy the stock, ask the broker to register the stock in your name rather than in the street name. Registration in the street name means that the stock you purchase is registered in the name of the brokerage firm rather than your name, required for most companies' DRIPs. Once you have purchased one share of stock, there are quite a few companies that will allow you to enroll in their DRIPs. You can then buy stocks directly from the companies and completely bypass the stockbroker and the huge commissions they normally charge, particularly for odd lots (stocks purchased in amounts of fewer than 100 shares per transaction). For example, if you purchased 5, 50, or 87 shares, you would be purchasing in an odd lot. Also, the companies who have DRIPs will reinvest the dividends you earn from their stock (see table below). This will eventually increase the value of your stock portfolios and could, given enough time, earn you another full share of the stock without your having to invest additional money from your pocket. Each year, you might be able to add stock from another company to diversify your portfolio.

Discount Brokers

Barry W. Murphy & Co.	(800) 221-2111
Charles Schwab & Co.	(800) 648-5300
Fidelity Brokerage Services	(800) 544-7272
Jack White & Co.	(800) 233-3411
Quick & Reilly Inc.	(800) 221-5220
Marquette de Bary Inc.	(800) 221-3305
Kennedy, Cabot and Company	(800) 252-0090

Some Companies Allowing Direct Purchases

Procter & Gamble	(800) 742-6253	Initial investment, $100
Regions Financial Corporation	(800) 638-6431	Initial investment, $500
Exxon Corporation	(800) 252-1800	Initial investment, $250
Duke Power	(800) 488-3853	Initial investment, $250

Companies with Dividend Reinvestment Programs

	Stock Price as of 12/1/95	52 Week High	52 Week Low	Yield	P/E Ratio
McDonald's Corporation (708) 575-3000 MCD	44 7/8	45 1/2	27 3/4	0.6	23.6
The Coca-Cola Company (404) 676-2121 KO	75 25/32	76 7/8	48 3/4	1.1	33
Johnson & Johnson (908) 524-0400 JNJ	85 7/8	87 1/4	57 1/8	1.5	23.9
Colgate-Palmolive Co. (212) 310-3207 CL	72 3/4	77 3/8	58	2.5	63.2
Proctor & Gamble PG (DIRECT Purchase)	84 3/4	89 1/2	60 1/2	1.8	21.9
Duke Power & Light DUK (DIRECT Purchase)	45 3/8	45 5/8	37 3/8	4.4	13.9
Regions Financial Corporation RGBK (DIRECT Purchase)	42 3/8	42 1/8	29 3/4	3.1	11.6

	Stock Price as of 12/1/95	52 Week High	52 Week Low	Yield	P/E Ratio
Exxon Corporation XON (DIRECT Purchase)	80 7/8	80 1/8	60 1/8	3.7	15
GTE Corporation (203) 965-2789 GTE	42 5/8	43 5/8	30	4.4	16.3
Honeywell Inc. (612) 870-5200 HON	47 1/2	49 1/2	28 1/4	2.1	19.4
Minnesota Power & Light (800) 535-3056 MPL	27 5/8	29 1/4	24 1/4	7.3	10.7
Minnesota Manufacturing & Mining Co. (3M) (612) 733-1110 MMM	65 1/4	66 1/4	50 3/4	2.8	19.4
PepsiCo Inc. (914) 253-2000 PEP	55 1/8	55 3/8	33 7/8	1.4	22.7
NationsBank Corp. (704) 386-7388 NB	71 3/4	73 7/8	43 3/8	3.2	10.6

Helpful Publications

Buying Stocks Without a Broker
Charles B. Carlson
McGraw-Hill, Inc.
1221 Avenue of the Americas
New York, NY 10020

No Load Stocks: How to Buy Your First Share and Every Share Directly from the Company with No Broker's Fee
Charles B. Carlson
McGraw-Hill, Inc.
1221 Avenue of the Americas
New York, NY 10020

INVESTMENT CLUBS

If you don't have enough money, you don't want to experiment with only your money, or you just want a little company in your investment ventures, consider starting an investment club. Investment clubs are groups of people who pool their money much like mutual fund investors and invest it collectively in stocks, bonds, and other investments. Consider asking some of your campus buddies or even a professor to join you in an investment adventure. You can research and choose your investments as a group, have more funds to invest, and—with any luck—get a nice return on your investment. For more information on establishing an investment club, contact the National Association of Investors Corporation (NAIC), 711 W. 13 Mile Road, Madison Heights, MI 48071, (810) 583-6242 or fax (810) 583-4880.

13

THE CREDIT CRUNCH

Credit can be a nightmare or a blessing for college students. Whether you are freshman just starting or a senior on the way out, you need to be aware of your credit options. As a college student you have easy and virtually instant access to a variety of credit and charge cards. As soon as you get a college ID and start receiving bills for your tuition, credit card companies begin to see you as a cash cow for the next four years—perhaps for the rest of your life.

You should understand that building a good credit rating is essential in our credit-based economy, and a credit card is one of the best ways to do that. Responsible use of a credit card and the timely paying of your monthly bills are easy ways to establish an excellent credit report, which will cause companies of all types to rush to offer you their services. On the flip side, if you abuse the privilege of having a credit card, it could haunt you for a long time and bring you a mountain of regrets. Your credit report will be very important when you purchase your first car, get an apartment in the city where you found your dream job, get a loan for a super business opportunity, or, down the road, when you purchase your first home. Some prospective employers may even consider your credit history, viewing it as a way to determine your maturity, responsibility, and preparation for doing a job. Having a bad credit history could destroy your chance at the job of your dreams.

Obtaining a credit card and building a good credit history will give you a jump start for managing your postgraduate financial life. During college, a credit card can come in handy when you have to buy a much-needed textbook for a difficult course or a suit for a very important job or internship interview but don't have cash on hand. There are many advantages to having credit and charge cards; however, it is essential that you use them wisely and responsibly because they can quickly become a great disadvantage if misused.

Common mistakes that college students make with their credit cards and credit history are:

- Being enticed by the representatives that credit card-issuing companies send to campus. Most of these representatives set up booths with free offerings like candy bars, hats, tee-shirts, cups, two-liter bottles of Coca-Cola, and so on. If you're hungry or thirsty after sitting through a two-hour lecture on ancient world history, these offerings of food and drink are often too good to resist. Your mind may have intelligently said, "No, you already have enough credit cards. If you get it, you might use it. You won't send it back," but your stomach wins with "I'm hungry. I don't care. Feed me now!" Before you know it, you've signed up for another credit card and your stomach is happy and quiet for the moment.
- Succumbing to the idea of obtaining cash discounts offered by department stores for completing an application for one of their credit cards. This is usually a one-time discount and does not apply to future purchases. Department store credit cards have some of the highest interest rates. The annual percentage rate (APR) for most is at least 20 percent or higher. Since you can use a VISA, MasterCard, American Express, or Discover card at most department and other stores, stick with them. Department store credit cards usually don't offer as many services or incentives as major credit card companies and their issuing banks do. At

most, they may offer free catalogs and advance notification of sales.

- Being unaware of the terms under which the credit card is offered. For example, whether the card has an annual fee or not, what is the interest rate, and so on.
- Letting the ease of having a credit card indulge him in overspending instead of comparison shopping or bargain hunting.
- Impulse buying of things she doesn't need just because the credit card is handy.
- Purchasing items on credit when cash is available. The student feels that he should have at least some cash handy, so he uses his credit card to keep the cash ready and available, not realizing that with a balance already on the card and a high interest rate, he could end up paying a lot more for the purchase than he would have with cash.
- Using a credit card for everyday expenditures and to pay bills such as buying snacks at a convenience store or paying the phone bill or the rent. Once a student starts using her cards for expenditures like these, she is probably digging a very big and black financial hole. If you don't need to use it for this, don't. If you need the money, you may need to find another, less expensive source for a short-term loan.
- Not paying credit card bills on time.
- Having too many credit cards. Numerous credit cards can create greater exposure to theft and loss for most individuals. If your wallet or purse is stolen, you may be liable for at least $50 of the amount the thief charges on your card. Also, with too many cards you may not remember all the credit cards you actually have and all the account numbers that you will have to replace them. Most cards now have credit card registries that you can use as a service to replace all the cards that you have registered with them. These services can cost as much as $50 for one year. It's really best to limit the number of cards you have and avoid this fee, which is money you could be investing.

I know someone who has fifteen credit cards and a debt of more than $10,000. He has student loans outstanding that will become payable approximately six months after he graduates. To put it simply, he is not in a good situation. By making mistakes like being easily enticed by offers from credit card companies and department stores, combined with the rest of the most common credit mistakes, he created a financial nightmare for himself. In his freshman year he began to obtain all types of credit cards, mainly to take advantage of the gifts, promotions, and cash discounts representatives were offering. He ended up with five major credit cards, including a Discover card, two Visas, and a MasterCard; five department store cards including those from Sears, JCPenney, Macy's, and Hecht's; and five gas cards, including Shell and Exxon. All of the cards carry a balance and interest rates ranging from 17.9 percent to almost 25 percent APR. All of the major credit cards had low introductory variable interest rates that were designed just for students. But after one year, most of them increased the interest rate to at least 12 percent, which is standard practice. When the economy and the prime rate started to rise last year, so did the interest rates. Most of them now hover around eighteen percent. Even though most of the remaining cards have fixed APRs, all of them are at least at 20 percent. This individual got into a major credit mess, which is going to haunt him for at least five years, or until he is able to pay off the high interest rate credit card debt. I hope you can see how this happened and how you can avoid and emerge from college debt free, or at least free of high interest rate credit card debt.

TERMS AND FEES YOU SHOULD KNOW

- Annual percentage rate (APR)—This is the interest you will be charged yearly. It is usually broken into a monthly periodic rate. To calculate the amount of interest you are paying when you make a payment, divide the APR by 12 to get the monthly periodic rate. Subtract the previous finance charges from your payment. Then multiply your balance subject to finance charges (which should be your previous balance less payments you made) by the monthly periodic rate. This gives you the actual amount you paid toward your balance. Most people who do this find that the majority of their payment was eaten up in finance charges. For example, suppose you had a balance of $2446.71. You make the minimum required payment of $50. Due to your interest rate, you have $37.28 in finance charges, so only $12.72 of the $50 paid actually goes to reduce your balance. This means that next month, your balance will be almost exactly the same, having been reduced only a fraction. In this instance, the balance was reduced by 0.5 percent, or less than 1 percent. At this rate, it would take years to pay off the balance, and that's with no new purchases!

- Variable rate—This means your interest rate fluctuates with the prime rate. Depending on the national economy, your interest rate could move up and down. At times you could have a low interest rate, and at others your interest rate could be very high.
- Grace period—The period of time you have before your credit card company starts charging interest on your new purchases. If you carry a balance you don't have a grace period. New purchases are added to the old balance and interest begins to accrue immediately. The only card that does not do this is the Optima "True Grace" card from American Express.
- Annual fee—Some companies charge you a yearly fee for the privilege of having their card in your possession. Even if you never use the card, you will still be charged the fee. For example, American Express charges an annual fee of $55.
- Cash advance fee—Fee for getting a cash advance (much like using an ATM) on your credit or charge card. Most cash advances are assessed a higher annual percentage rate than regular purchases on the card. The company also

begins charging interest from the day you receive the cash—there is no grace period.

- Company-issued credit card—Issued by individual organizations such as oil companies (Shell, Exxon), major department stores (JCPenney, Macy's) and other retailers. These cards can be used only to purchase items at the issuing company. For example, your Structure card can be used only at Structure or its affiliates. Most of these cards will allow you to make a minimum monthly payment on your total balance. This is called a revolving balance. Because most company-issued cards charge interest rates ranging from 18 percent to as high as 24 percent carrying a balance with these cards can become very expensive.
- Travel and entertainment charge card (sometimes called convenience cards)—Cards that fall into this category are American Express, Diners Club, Carte Blanche, and the like. These cards usually allow you to have a high or unlimited credit line, based on your individual purchases, your ability to pay, and past expenditures. However, these cards usually require that your balance be paid in full within 30 days of the statement date. They do not charge interest during this period, but if the balance is not paid, they will charge a penalty, which can range from $10 to $20, or 2.5 percent of the balance due. The majority of these cards also offer additional features, such as product warranties and travel insurance. Most of them charge an annual fee. The best reason to have one of these cards is as a safeguard against overspending. If you know you *must* pay your bill in full when you receive the statement, then the temptation to buy something you cannot afford will not be as great and may even fade away as you face the possibility of a stiff penalty.
- Third party credit cards—These cards are issued by financial institutions such as banks and credit unions, in association with Visa and MasterCard. These cards are the most common and widely used. These cards may or may not

charge an annual fee. They allow revolving balances and have interest rates ranging from 9 percent to 20 percent, depending on the issuing institution. If you plan to pay off your balance in full each month, you won't have to worry about the interest rate. If you don't, find one with the lowest interest rate possible.

It is also important to remember that credit cards allow to you to purchase based on an established line of credit. You can carry a balance. Charge cards allow you only to "buy now, pay later." Later is when they send you the bill. You cannot carry a balance.

CREDIT AND CARDS

The following are credit and charge cards that generally cater to college students by offering additional services such as magazine and telephone discounts, low airfares, and other attractive options (subject to change).

- Citibank Visa or MasterCard—Offers savings on airfare— up to $25 off domestic flights with no blackout dates or usage limits, to any destination, at any time. You can also save up to 24 percent off long-distance calls with MCI. Other features include insurance protection for purchased items, no cosigner or minimum income needed, magazine programs, price protection, and extended warranties.
- Discover Card—Offers basically the same services to students who are enrolled in college as to regular Discover card holders. Typically only upperclass students are approved for this card. The benefits of this card include no annual fee, the Smart Rate program, and a 1 percent cash back bonus award based on your annual level of purchases.
- AT&T Universal MasterCard—This card is advertised as a three-in-one card. It combines all the features of a credit card, ATM card, and a calling card. Although it sounds like

a great deal, several cards offered by major banks issuing credit cards offer the same features. In fact, American Express, a charge card, can be used to obtain instant cash through its Express Cash programs and can be used as a calling card through MCI. Likewise, Citibank offers a credit card with 24-hour access to cash, as well as calling card features through MCI.

- American Express—This charge card offers student savings on airfare through Continental Airlines; on long-distance phone calls through MCI, including thirty minutes of free long distance each year; and discounts for products from J. Crew, American Express, Software, Inc., and many others.

You should definitely shop around for the credit or charge card that will best meet your needs. Ultimately, you want to have the least amount of credit cards to serve the greatest portion of your needs and make the smallest possible hole in your pocket in terms of interest and annual fees. You may want to consult one of the following organizations to obtain a listing of low interest rate and no-fee credit cards, as well as other booklets and services for the responsible use of credit and credit cards.

Bankcard Holders of America
560 Herndon Parkway, Suite 120
Herndon, VA 22070   (800) 553-8025

- For a small fee, offers several information booklets and listings of no-fee/low-rate credit cards, secured credit cards, and other reports.

Consumer Credit Card Rating Service
PO Box 5483
Oxnard, CA 93031   (310) 392-7720

- Compares thousands of credit cards on the basis of their annual fees, benefits, grace periods, and other features. There is a fee for this service.

Ram Research/Publishing Company
Box 1700 (College Estates)
Frederick, MD 21701   (800) 344-7714

- Tracks U.S. bank cards. Offers several publications devoted to consumers and their credit card needs.

YOUR CREDIT REPORT

You should get a copy of your credit report every year—request it. Sometimes mistakes can be made by organizations that issue credit. They may report incorrect information to national credit reporting agencies such as Equifax and TRW. Monitoring your credit report can result in early detection of these mistakes; you can quickly clear them off your record. Doing so will ensure that when you need additional credit or a prospective employer checks your credit history, you will know that it's in good shape. You can request a free copy of your credit report by calling TRW at (800) 682-7654.

14

OTHER OPPORTUNITIES

There are countless opportunities open to you in college; I have discussed many of them throughout this book. Others, such as exchange programs, conferences, contests, and honors programs, will be discussed in this final chapter. Many of the opportunities I have introduced to you may be unique and may not currently exist on your campus. However, that doesn't mean you can't take advantage of them. You can still participate, either by working with someone at your college or university to get the program started, or by participating in a program or opportunity offered by another college or university. Find someone at your university who is receptive to your ideas and work with them. In many cases, a program or opportunity may already exist without students being aware of it. Ask around and be observant—that's how I found out about most of the opportunities and programs I have written about. Of course I couldn't cover everything in one book, and your school may well have unique programs, but I hope you've gotten a taste of what's out there.

UNIVERSITY EXCHANGE PROGRAMS

Are you tired of your university? Want to try out a new one? Get involved with an exchange program and trade places with another student. University exchange programs allow students of one school to study at another within the United States or abroad. Usually the institutions are similar in their educational styles and traditions. For example, students at Spelman College can study at similar institutions like Mount Holyoke, Vassar, and Wellesley. Also Rhodes College in Memphis, Tennessee, has direct exchange programs with Eberhard-Karls University Tübingen in Germany and Kansai University in Japan. Students of Rhodes College can attend either institution for a year without paying extra tuition. This type of program allows you to explore the curriculum and traditions of another educational institution, take courses that your university may not offer, or attend the class of a world famous professor or renowned author who teaches at that school.

UNIVERSITY HIGHLIGHTS
SPELMAN COLLEGE

Spelman College, a black women's college in Atlanta, Georgia, offers its students numerous enhancement programs. Among them are exchange programs with colleges including Wellesley, Mount Holyoke, Vassar, and Mills. Spelman also maintains an honors program and its students attend professional conferences all over the country. Its alumnae–student externship allows students to observe Spelman alumnae in their chosen professions. During the summer, Spelman students can take advantage of the Women in Science Engineering Program, which allows students to work at NASA headquarters.

BELOIT COLLEGE

Beloit College in Beloit, Wisconsin, offers its students a summer employment program, school-arranged jobs, and internships. Through its World Outlook Program, study opportunities abroad are plentiful, particularly in countries such as China, Ecuador, Hungary, Japan, and Turkey. There are also special problems courses allowing students in small groups or individually to work with professors on research projects. In the Fudan-Beloit Exchange programs, five students and a faculty member exchange places with five students and a faculty member at Fudan University in China.

DOUBLE MAJOR

Can't make up your mind about the area you want to major in? Declare a major in two subjects. Most universities will allow students to complete the requirements of two majors at the same time. If you are interested in having a diverse skill base, a double major is an excellent opportunity for you. Your majors could be totally dissimilar, such as French and computer science, or complementary, such as French and international relations. It might take you a little longer to graduate and it will certainly require more effort, but if you think it's for you, go for it!

A MINOR

A minor is a program of study in which a student takes a number of courses in a discipline that are not enough to be a major, but are more than other courses. A minor is usually a secondary interest to the major. For example, if a student majors in accounting, she could minor in Spanish—the two don't have to be related. The minor generally shows on your academic transcript.

In many instances, college graduates have entered professions in the area of their minor rather than their major—our student might go on to be a Spanish instructor rather than an accountant. In any case, minors give students the opportunity to explore other areas of interest.

3-2, 3-1, 2-2 PROGRAMS

3-2, 3-1, and 2-2 are cooperative academic programs involving two postsecondary institutions. For example, in a 3-2 program, you would study at one institution for three years, then transfer to the second for two years. A 2-2 program involves equal amounts of time at each institution; a 3-1 program involves three years at one institution and one at another. For instance, Loyola University in Chicago, Illinois, has a 3-2 engineering program with the University of Illinois at Urbana-Champaign.

CONTESTS

Thoughts . . .
drifting aimlessly
through deep dark regions
A glimmer of light
rushes in and fades away
to join the others that have long been forgotten
Quickly,
another flickers into
the powerhouse that is my mind
only to slink stealthily back
unworthy
of further notice

Another
bursts forth in a mushroom of clearness.
I have it!
A sound thought
worthy of notice
worthy of praise
and worthy of me.

I submitted this poem to the National Library of Poetry as part of a contest. It was selected as a finalist and published in the library's national anthology of poetry, *The Dark Side of the Moon*. It was also included on an audiotape.

Throughout your college career, you will have many opportunities to participate in contests or competitions. Take advantage of every opportunity, even if it isn't necessarily an area of expertise for you. Entering competitions allows you to get feedback on your efforts, which can help you to improve yourself and discover skills in which you didn't know you were proficient. Whether you win or lose, competitions can also add spice to your résumé or the personal statement on your graduate school application. Your competitive experiences will help to form an image of a highly motivated individual in the minds of prospective employers or admissions officers.

Moreover, your participation in competitions and contests could get exposure for you and some of your pursuits, particularly those that need funding. Winners of the All USA Academic Team competition described at the end of the chapter, are highlighted in a special edition of USA Today, a national newspaper. Their photographs and a small synopsis of their endeavors are printed in the newspaper. If you need national exposure for a charity, research effort, or some other endeavor, this is a good way to get it.

Other potential benefits of contests are prize money and free trips, such as the one David Buckholtz, a student at Emory University, took when he was selected as a winner of the international essay competition organized by the international students committee at Harvard University. He describes it: "Last spring I was selected as a finalist in the ISC symposium essay contest, which allowed me to visit St. Gallen, Switzerland, for free. . . . The conference was an amazing experience, especially being there with other scholars, but the highlight of my trip was the chance to take some time before the conference and travel around Europe. It was my first trip out of the Eastern time zone, not to mention the United States." Travel opportunities are frequently part of worldwide, national, or sometimes even regional competitions.

Contests abound on college campuses all over the world. You can participate in poetry, oratorical, debating, mock trial team, photography, dance, essay, music, and many other types of competitions. Get involved and compete! Competition stimulates your mind and helps you get into practice for the competitiveness of just being alive.

To find out about competitions which you might like to enter, read your campus newspaper and other magazines for college students, or consult your major department. Your dean's and president's offices may be familiar with other competitions.

All USA Academic Team Competition
c/o Carol Skalski
1000 Wilson Blvd
Arlington, VA 22229   (703) 276-5890

- A competition based on achievements and the recommendation of your university and sponsored by *USA Today*, a national newspaper. Winners are featured in the newspaper and those on the first team are awarded $2,500 and an all-expense-paid trip to Washington, D.C., to attend the American Council on Education convention.

Global Youth Exchange Program
Consulate General of Japan
80 SW 8th Street, Suite 3200
Miami, FL 33149

- A program designed to promote mutual international understanding. Discussions are held on various prominent national and international issues. Winners are selected by essay and their supporting application documents. They receive an all-expense-paid two-week trip to Japan.

International Management Symposium
ISC-USA
Harvard University
PO Box 382886
Cambridge, MA 02238

- International essay competition sponsored by McKinsey & Co. Winners go to St. Gallen, Switzerland, and participate in the International Management Symposium. The symposium is attended by international leaders in industry, government, academia, and finance. Participants can share their views on the international theme during workshops, panels, and lectures.

National Library of Poetry
11419 Cronridge Drive
PO Box 704-ZK
Owings Mills, MD 21117

- Annual national poetry contest sponsored by the National Library of Poetry.

Who's Who Among Students in American
    Universities and Colleges
3200 Rice Mine Rd., NE
PO Box 2029
Tuscaloosa, AL 35403

- Recognition program based on the nomination of your school. Contact your student activities or dean's offices for more information on nomination procedures. You may

have to complete an application and submit an essay or recommendations before being nominated by your university
or college for this award.

HONORS PROGRAMS

Honors programs are designed to provide challenging courses
and extracurricular activities for high-achieving students and to
encourage academic excellence. Some advantages of membership in the honors program (depending on the college) are:

- Possible acceleration in the completion of your general
  studies requirements
- Enrollment in classes of reduced size
- Opportunities for the development of leadership skills
  through honors activities
- Individual honors courses and completion of honors program requirements will be listed on your transcript
- Participation in state, regional, and national meetings of
  honors councils
- Honors seminars—for example, Presbyterian College of
  South Carolina offers its honors program members the
  opportunity to participate in the honors seminar in great
  ideas, the dean's seminar for freshman, departmental
  honors research, and the honors seminar in great books.

I participated in the University Honors Program at Florida
A & M University for the duration of my undergraduate career.
Our advisor, Ivy Mitchell, encouraged participation in numer-
ous honors council conferences all over the United States.
Under her direction, we organized the first and second annual
Bernard D. Hendricks Undergraduate Honors Conferences.
Honors program activities helped me develop my leadership,
motivational, and teamwork skills. Not only were we made
aware of honors-related activities, but we were encouraged to

participate in many national contests and programs. Members were also involved in several community service projects that involved mentoring and tutoring students in high school.

INTERDISCIPLINARY PROGRAMS

Interdisciplinary programs allow students to study or learn about a variety of subjects through classes, seminars, and workshops. In an interdisciplinary program, you are able to get a more broad education, because you can fully experience two or more subjects. These programs are designed by university departments to provide a grouping of courses or projects taken from various disciplines and focused around a specific theme. You will also become more well-rounded, with familiarity in several fields of study rather than just one.

UNIVERSITY HIGHLIGHTS

Students at Boston College in Chestnut Hill, Massachusetts, have many unique extracurricular experiences to choose from. The college emphasizes interdisciplinary programs in its quest to produce well-rounded students with a holistic view of the world. The interdisciplinary programs of study include American Studies, Environmental Affairs and International Studies. One program, PULSE, is run by students for students and helps them get involved in social and field service work while satisfying their course requirements for philosophy and theology. Students can also participate in immersion and honors programs.

For students in the chemical engineering department of New Mexico State University in Las Cruces, New Mexico, interdisciplinary teamwork is a key element of their education. The interdisciplinary program has four broad areas:

environmental engineering, advanced materials, food engineering and biochemical engineering. An example of the interdisciplinary research and education projects in which students are involved under the biochemical engineering interdisciplinary program are algae conservation for waste water treatment with the chemistry department and development of control systems for growth chambers with the biology department. The chemical engineering department also operates a 75-liter fermenter in cooperation with the chemistry department.

EARLY ADMISSION PROGRAMS

Degree programs at certain professional schools will allow some pre-professional students to enroll immediately after their junior year at an undergraduate school. These are usually programs in business, law, and medical schools and are reserved for students who show exceptional talent and have impressive academic records. With this option you can either shorten the usual time needed to earn both undergraduate and graduate degrees from a professional school, or you can guarantee your eventual admission to the school early and begin preparing for those studies early. Loyola University in Chicago, Illinois, has a 3-3 Law Program offered in conjunction with their School of Law. This program allows students to enter law school after three years of undergraduate work.

CONFERENCES/FORUMS

Conferences are formal meetings usually arranged by an association for the benefit of its countrywide member chapters. These meetings involve panel discussions with experts on topics of interest to the members. They may also include self-help workshops on areas such as managing finances, developing good study habits, and managing time wisely. There is always at least one keynote speaker, usually a recognized expert in the field or an author.

The benefits of attending conferences are numerous. As an attendee, you can absorb ideas from other students, converse with experts from diverse fields, develop a network of contacts, listen to inspiring speakers, and take home new information to apply to your life. At many of the conferences I attended, members of the organization were given the opportunity to present and lead sessions in keeping with the theme of that year's conference. This is an excellent way to develop your presentation and public speaking skills. Also, if you're interested in graduate school, these conferences are good ways to expand your ideas and opinions in a particular field, since most of the presentations are based on an individual's own research in an area.

You don't necessarily have to be a member to attend an organization's conference, since many require all attendees to pay a fee to come anyway. As a nonmember you can pay a fee as well, although it is usually higher. The conferences you would be interested in attending as a college student might even be paid for by your university, as mine were.

I attended many conferences while at FAMU. They were in interesting cities including San Antonio, St. Louis, and Washington. Exploring the city is an added bonus after you've attended several sessions during the day. Tours were usually arranged for those who wanted to explore as a group.

One of the most memorable experiences of my undergraduate years was attending a conference sponsored by the National Collegiate Honors Council. At this conference several notable speakers gave presentations, but in my opinion, the best and most inspirational was the writer Nikki Giovanni. Her excellent speech touched on many of today's important issues. Although speaking on these issues is not unique to her, as many speakers touch upon them at some point for emphasis and impact, the excellence of her talk stemmed from her ability to relate her viewpoint in a humorous yet soulful and touching manner. I wanted to laugh, cry, and scream all at once. Giovanni talked about growing old, race relations, family, love, and a host of other topics. Her comments were extremely well presented and focused, even though they covered a spectrum of ideas. To this day, she ranks as one of the best speakers I have ever heard.

UNIVERSITY HIGHLIGHTS THE DEVELOPMENTAL TRANSCRIPT PROGRAM AT GEORGE MASON UNIVERSITY

George Mason University in Fairfax, Virginia, gives its students the opportunity to build an official transcript of activities and out-of-classroom learning experiences. The transcript can be used as an official accompaniment to include with academic transcripts when students apply for jobs or admission to graduate school. The program gives students the opportunity to structure their out-of-class learning experiences such as workshops and learning programs into more organized and meaningful documented experiences. Students can also network with others in the developmental transcript program who have already participated in the activities in which they are interested.

All I Really Need to Know about Life I Learned in Kindergarten by Robert Fulghum hit home with many people. In my opinion, everything you need to know about life you'll learn in college—if you learned it in kindergarten, you'll learn it all over again. This time it will mean something, unlike when you were a six-year-old and your biggest worry was how to wheedle another chocolate chip cookie from your mother, or how to open up your presents before Christmas without your parents' finding out. In college you will learn how to cooperate, commiserate, educate, manipulate, plead, grovel, laugh, and so much more. Everything you learn, good or bad, will enrich you as an adult and prepare you for the rest of life's journey. Whether your experiences delight or disgust you, college is an overall educational experience. Make sure not to skip any part of it. No one likes disappointment and pain, but sometimes we all have to put up with both to experience life fully. If you work hard to get the most out of your college education, you will not be disappointed.

College should not be undertaken solely to get a degree—go to college to get an education by taking advantage of opportunities. Many opportunities will lie directly in your path while you're in college. Watch out—opportunity could be knocking at your door at any moment. Will you be ready? For those of you who believe that you should focus only on getting a degree, understand that the majority of college graduates don't work in the field in which they obtained their degree. Instead, they are usually in a field they happened on by accident or that they nurtured as a sideline interest in college. If you, the reader, use this book to help get the most of your college experience, you will enjoy a richer life, both during and after college. If you're thinking about going to college or are already in college, make the most of it. You won't regret it!

Index